A DARK HISTORY:
CATHOLIC CHURCH

T. J 669.

A DARK HISTORY:
CATHOLIC CHURCH

SCHISMS, WARS, INQUISITIONS, WITCH HUNTS, SCANDALS, CORRUPTION

MICHAEL KERRIGAN

METRO BOOKS
New York

METRO BOOKS
New York

An Imprint of Sterling Publishing
387 Park Avenue South
New York, NY 10016

Editorial and design by
Amber Books Ltd
74–77 White Lion Street
London N1 9PF
www.amberbooks.co.uk

Project Editor: Michael Spilling
Designer: Jerry Williams
Picture Research: Terry Forshaw

ISBN: 978-1-4351-5195-6

For information about custom editions, special sales, and premium and corporate purchases,
please contact Sterling Special Sales at 800-805-5489 or specialsales@sterlingpublishing.com.

Manufactured in China

2 4 6 8 10 9 7 5 3 1

www.sterlingpublishing.com

CONTENTS

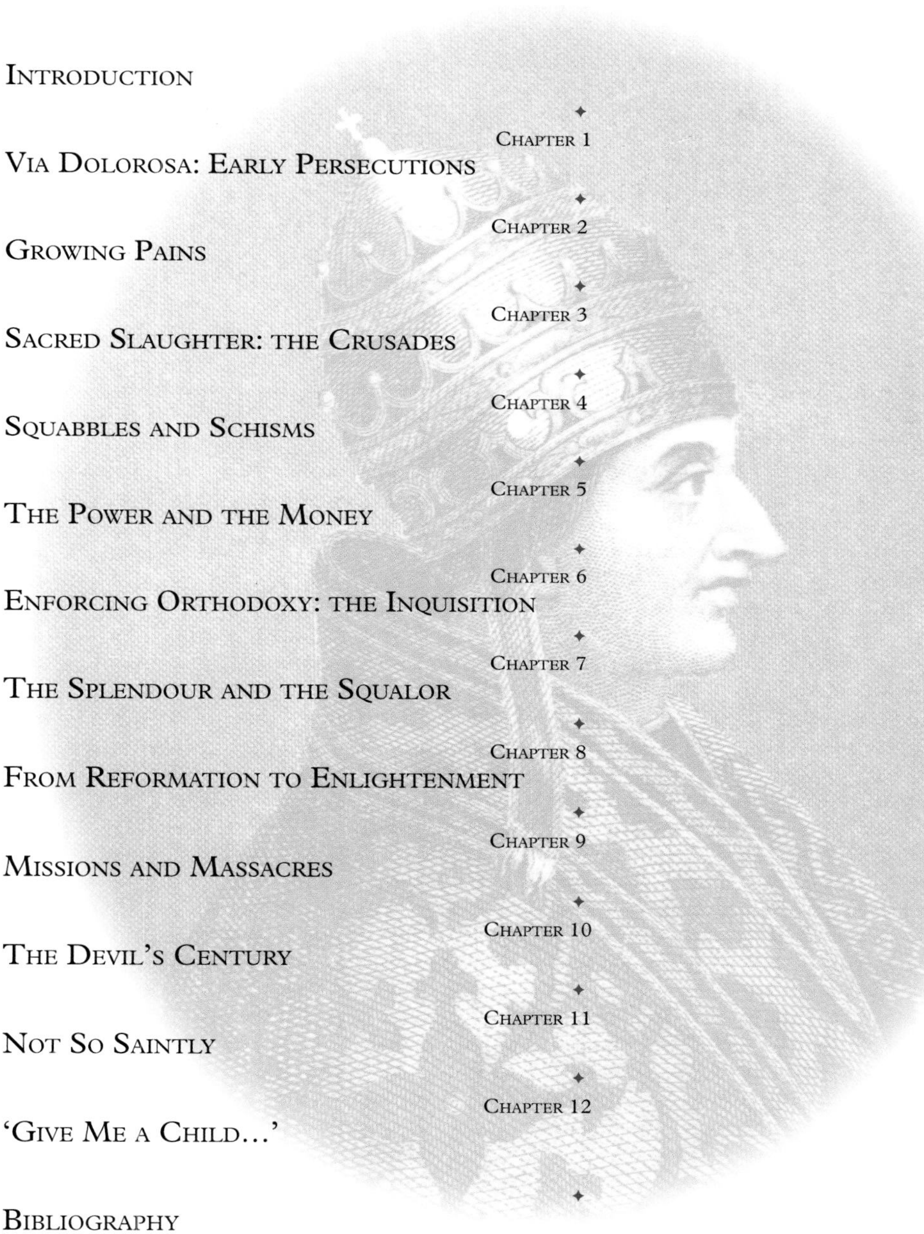

Introduction   6

CHAPTER 1

VIA DOLOROSA: EARLY PERSECUTIONS   14

CHAPTER 2

GROWING PAINS   26

CHAPTER 3

SACRED SLAUGHTER: THE CRUSADES   36

CHAPTER 4

SQUABBLES AND SCHISMS   62

CHAPTER 5

THE POWER AND THE MONEY   80

CHAPTER 6

ENFORCING ORTHODOXY: THE INQUISITION   92

CHAPTER 7

THE SPLENDOUR AND THE SQUALOR   112

CHAPTER 8

FROM REFORMATION TO ENLIGHTENMENT   134

CHAPTER 9

MISSIONS AND MASSACRES   148

CHAPTER 10

THE DEVIL'S CENTURY   170

CHAPTER 11

NOT SO SAINTLY   196

CHAPTER 12

'GIVE ME A CHILD...'   210

BIBLIOGRAPHY   218

INDEX   219

PICTURE CREDITS   224

INTRODUCTION

When it comes to Catholicism, there's no shortage of material for a 'dark history' – some readers will wonder whether there is any other kind. An understandable reaction, perhaps even justifiable, but it's not the business of this book to offer some sort of divine 'Last Judgment' on the Church.

'See … the Son of Man is betrayed into the hands of sinners.'

Does St Francis's Sermon to the Birds signify more than Pius IX's strictures against democracy? How would you weigh the Sistine Chapel against child abuse? Notre Dame against the crimes of the Crusaders? Which should matter more in the scheme of things: the incredible courage the Church inspired in its many martyred believers, or its wholesale torture and execution of its foes? What of those nuns and priests who played their part in saving Jewish families from destruction in the Holocaust? Can their heroism counterbalance the Vatican's reluctance to condemn? How, to take a more down-to-

Opposite: Missionaries of Charity in Kolkata commemorate the anniversary of their founder's death. Mother Teresa exemplified Catholicism at its best and worst. More worldly than she seemed; more selective in her love, more ruthless in her actions, she nevertheless inspired a great many to good works.

earth example from contemporary life, do you weigh the work of a nursing sister in an African hospice against the Church's refusal to countenance the use of condoms in the fight against AIDS? And what would it matter, others may ask, if Catholicism had done no end of good, if the whole historical evidence is founded on a lie?

We're never going to agree. Mother Teresa has become a case in point, fast-tracked for sainthood by the Church to the bemusement of liberal sceptics for whom she's been exposed – emphatically and repeatedly – as a charlatan. Even if all the criticisms against her are true, it might be argued that the inspiration she's given others more than offsets any harm she's done – or good she's failed to do. At the very least she was a walking, talking feel-good factor: in a famous 1988 study, Harvard students shown movie-footage of Mother Teresa ministering to the sick registered a measurable rise in IgA (Immunoglobulin A) levels. In other words, she did something beautiful for their immune systems – a miracle of the psychological placebo effect, if not of God.

A Catholic Cosmos

The Church is too big and complex to be characterized as any one thing: the dogmatism with which it speaks is in this sense misleading. '*Roma locate est, causa finita est*', said St Augustine, simply – 'Rome has spoken, the case is closed' – but Rome itself is much more ambiguous than it seems. Its sheer size precludes straightforwardness. When they called it the Catholic (or 'universal') Church, they may have been exaggerating, but not by much. It's hard to think of any historic institution that can compare. The hegemony of Egypt's pharaohs may have lasted several times longer, but it extended over only a relatively tiny patch of Earth. The U.S. presidency might surpass it now both in influence and reach, but the United States has been a world power for only a matter of decades, and a 'full-spectrum dominance' for only a few years.

While in some ways it may seem absurd to judge a religion by the same standards as a secular state, Catholicism isn't just any religion; isn't just any *world* religion even. 'How many divisions has the Pope?' asked a scornful Stalin. And he had a point – well into the nineteenth century the Papal States had been a temporal realm, with a real army. Even since that time, through a century or so in which its authority has been 'merely' spiritual, it's had a major – sometimes decisive – role in world affairs.

And, as the Church is quick to remind us, its power isn't limited to this world. 'Whatever you bind on Earth shall be bound in heaven. Whatever you loose on Earth shall be loosed in heaven,' Christ told St Peter (Matthew 18: 18). Protestants may dispute the Church's interpretation of the verse – as *carte blanche* for world religious domination – and atheists dispute the very premise on which it's founded, but there is really no doubt that Catholicism is conceived on an unimaginably awe-inspiring scale. If its structures transcend our Earthly existence (or are at least supposed to), it claims as a community of souls to bring together not just the living but the righteous dead. Alongside the 'Church Militant', fighting the good fight in this world, there's the 'Church Suffering'

Opposite: Christ sits in judgment, as imagined by an artist of the fourteenth-century School of Rimini. How would the Saviour think His Church has done? 'Feed my sheep,' said Jesus (John 21: 17), but has the Catholic Church been a Good Shepherd – or a self-serving institution?

Above: St Theresa of Lisieux, the 'Little Flower', has inspired and cheered millions with her simple faith and her down-to-earth approach to Christian life. But her childlike ingenuousness isn't an adequate basis for the building of a world religion: how is Catholicism to keep its innocence?

in purgatory, awaiting our prayers for their salvation, and the 'Church Triumphant' with God and the saints in heaven. Covering an infinity of space and an eternity of time, and bringing together billions in its congregation, the Catholic Church is the vastest of institutions.

The Inner Life

And yet, at the same time, it's one that has touched the most intimate lives of its believers, for better and for worse, occupying their innermost psychic space with its spiritual assumptions and moral laws. While this has meant mystic ecstasy for some, for others it's spelled

GUILTY AS CHARGED?

THE VIEW THAT Catholics have to carry round with them a crippling sense of guilt is a relatively new one. British travellers in Italy, from Byron and Shelley to E.M. Forster, came away enraptured at the carefree attitudes they found. While some attributed this to sunshine, warm-bloodedness and an essentially childlike ingenuousness, others identified a religious cause. As Catholics, the reasoning went, Italians could basically get up to anything they liked all week, then confess on Saturday and have their sins wiped clean. Since Italianness and Catholicism were equally alien to these visitors, we don't know how far they distinguished between the two. The 'carefree Catholic' stereotype may be rooted in that same condescending view of the ethnic 'Other' that was to produce the grinning black minstrel figure a little later.

The Irish haven't escaped such stereotyping – that excruciating 'top o' the morning' cheeriness – but where religion's concerned, they have been taken more seriously. Irish Catholicism (and what are taken to be its derived forms in Britain, Australasia and North America) is assumed to bring with it a well-nigh unbearable burden of guilt. Some have attributed this to Jansenism. The theology of Cornelius Jansen (1585–1638) took from the works of St Augustine the conviction that man was born all but irredeemably steeped in sin. Without direct divine intervention, he was damned. Jansenism was taken up with morose enthusiasm in seventeenth-century France. So close did it come to complete despair, though, that it was condemned as heresy and suppressed. The suggestion is that it didn't disappear completely but – taken back by young seminarians – endured in Ireland.

A persuasive theory – or it would be if it were actually supported by any historical evidence. Then again, there's only the sketchiest evidence that Irish (or any other) 'Catholic Guilt' exists at all. A UC Berkeley/Notre Dame survey of U.S. teenagers could find no evidence that the Catholics were abnormally tormented. The issue remains unresolved.

Below: Lord Byron in nineteenth-century Rome, for him a playground of pleasure – the perfect antidote to an uptight England. Such differences, if they exist at all, are likely to be cultural and contextual – there's little evidence that Catholics feel more or less guilty than other people.

sexual repression and an all but paralyzing sense of sinfulness. The idea of 'Catholic Guilt' may be a cliché, but can we be sure it's without foundation? Any more than we can understand the (equally glib) contention that Catholicism can see women only as 'virgins' or as 'whores'? That one who's 'born a Catholic' is 'scarred for life', his or her identity determined – regardless of conscious theological (dis)beliefs – may be an exaggeration, but is it really so completely devoid of truth?

This book can do no more than hint at that darker dimension of Catholic history which has acted itself out in the tormented consciences of unhappy individuals over centuries. That the same set of values has buoyed up the spirits of St Theresa of Lisieux, fortified the courage of St Joan and transported St John of the Cross to religious rapture, perhaps only underlines a deep ambivalence at the heart of the Catholic Church and faith.

Above: John Paul II is welcomed by joyous crowds on his visit to Ireland in 1979: this 'rock-star pope' gave the Church a new and friendly face. Behind the scenes, though, Catholicism was as austere as ever in its moral teachings; and often, as hypocritical as ever in its own affairs.

Successions, Failures

Our main preoccupation here has to be the Church's changing role in a changing world – and this is an enormous subject in itself. Dip into Catholicism's history and you'll find what's supposed to be a story of seamless continuity – of 'apostolic succession' – a narrative of rifts and crises, of fits and starts. At the outset, a tiny Jewish sect; then a minority-cult in imperial Rome; and in medieval Europe the keeper of an unquestioned world-view. From this time on, the apostolic succession was beset by a series of opposing forces, from rival Christianities through secular scepticism to twentieth-century totalitarianism – and

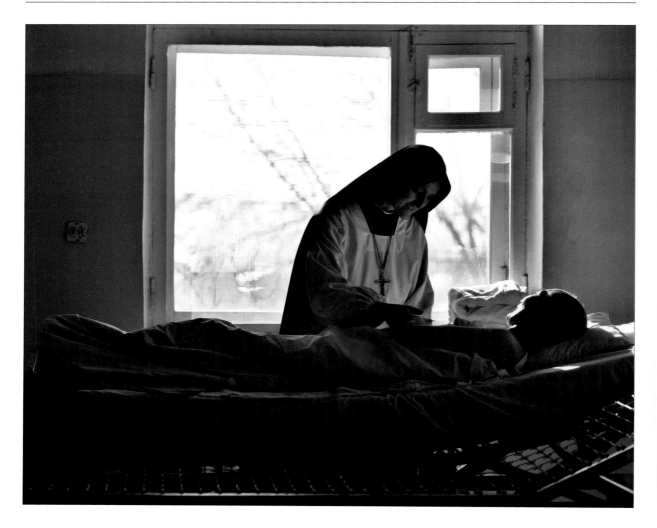

finally to consumerism in our own time. Even at its strongest, the Catholic Church has shown itself again and again to be all too flawed. No Catholic would seriously suggest taking the life of Alexander VI as a model; few would dispute that the first 'infallible' Pope, Pius IX, was personally to prove very fallible indeed. Conversely, it's often been in its times of greatest apparent weakness that the Church has shown most integrity, all the way through from the Roman catacombs to Communist Poland.

Changing Times, Changing Church

Perspective is all, of course: one commentator's 'inconsistency' is another one's 'flexibility'; what seems 'monolithic' to one man may be admirably 'coherent' for another. Down the centuries, in fact, the Catholic

Above: Sister Marie Benedict tends a patient in a hospital run by the French Fraternité de Notre Dame in Mongolia. All around the world, men and women are devoting their lives to others with single-minded heroism, inspired to do so by their Catholic faith.

Church has proven much more adaptable than might be imagined – or, as one might see it, much more willing to trim and tack to the prevailing wind. What sound like they should be fundamental 'truths' have simply been dropped into the religious mix at intervals – the idea of Purgatory in the sixth century and that of Papal Infallibility not until the nineteenth century. 'Heretics' went to the stake in the sixteenth century for introducing the sort of vernacular scripture that Catholicism would introduce itself in the twentieth. Much more constant, a cynic might say, has been the

SACRED SECRETS

THERE ARE OVER 50 miles of shelving in the Vatican's Secret Archives; 35,000 volumes in the catalogue alone. Much remains unavailable – a 75-year quarantine rule means that scholars have only recently had access to documents dating from World War II. As for earlier material, nothing will convince the determined conspiracy theorist that the Church isn't covering up the marriage of Jesus and Mary Magdalen and lord knows what else, but the reality is mostly more mundane. In a post-*Da Vinci Code* spasm of transparency, though, the Archive has released a range of items. A petition from England's nobles asking Clement VII for the annulment of Henry VIII's marriage to Catherine of Aragon; the proceedings of the trial of Galileo; Leo X's decree excommunicating Martin Luther... There's nothing here we didn't know about, but this is the real stuff of history, more intriguing than any fantasy could be.

Church's tendency to speak flatteringly to power and to take the side of wealth and rank in any struggle with the people.

The criticism is by no means wholly fair, but it comes a great deal too close for comfort: many within the Church would admit as much. A more charitable view would acknowledge the difficulties facing any movement that hopes to make a difference in the real world without at the same time compromising its ideals. Again, it's a matter of point-of-view: do we focus on the dedication and courage of so many ordinary priests and nuns and members of the laity in the face of hardship and danger down the centuries or on the excesses and hypocrisies of the hierarchy?

In the end, perhaps, it all comes down to a conclusion that the Church would recognize itself: in so far as its domain is in this world, it's human – flawed, and susceptible to sin. And how, we might marvel, thinking of all those cruel Inquisitors, those promiscuous Popes, those stampers-out of science and culture, those defenders of dictators, those abusers of children and exploiters of the poor. Yet it has to be admitted that there's another side to the Church as well. Whether or not we accept its claims to have a truly transcendent, heavenly dimension, there's no doubt that many of its members have done much good.

Right: Archivist Monsignor Martino Giusti shows Princeton's Professor Kenneth M. Setton a fifteenth-century treaty between the Roman and the Byzantine Churches. Catholicism has had a long and rich – and uniquely well-documented – history. Yet it has by no means been exclusively a force for good.

VIA DOLOROSA: EARLY PERSECUTIONS

'I am the way, the truth and the life,' Jesus promised his disciples – but the cruelty of his Passion was to bring them a clear warning: the Christian faithful could expect to endure great suffering and loss.

◆

'Take this cup of suffering from me.'
— *MARK, 14: 26*

The rich young man instructed to give away all his possessions to the poor; the outraged citizens told to think of their own sins before they attacked the adulteress; the victim of violence ordered to 'turn the other cheek' … Christ's first followers were left in little doubt that, although their faith would ultimately bring them to Everlasting Life, it would cost them – perhaps very considerably – in the here and now. Indeed, whatever joy it brought, the road to Salvation was inevitably going to lead

Opposite: Aelbert Bouts' fifteenth-century altarpiece suggests the brutal violence behind a faith which was founded in the sufferings of its Saviour. Christ's disciples, in the early centuries, knew that their own fate was unpredictable; that they themselves might easily come to grisly ends.

them through deep and difficult vales of darkness and death. The story of the early Church was to be no different. By 312, Christianity would be basking in the backing of the state, the official religion of the Roman world. First, though, there were terrible persecutions to be endured.

The First Martyrs
The radiance of the Resurrection fading, Christ's Ascension quickly coming to seem more like an abandonment, the darkness wasn't long in falling for the followers of Christ. The first known martyrdom – the stoning to death of St Stephen in Jerusalem around AD 35 – was witnessed by the future St Paul. Then still known as Saul, a young man from Tarsus in the province of Cilicia (southern Turkey), he was as proud of his Roman citizenship as of his Jewish background. Stephen's stand appeared an affront to both. So much so that, far from objecting to what amounted to a religious lynching, Saul stood by and

minded the cloaks of the killers as they hurled their stones at Stephen. Later, of course, his attitudes were to be transformed by the extraordinary experience he underwent on the Road to Damascus. Now named Paul, he became co-founder with St Peter of what we now know as the creed of Christianity. And while Peter may have been Christ's anointed Pope, Paul was arguably more important in building the Catholic Church: it was under his influence that it transcended its origins as a Jewish sect.

> Nero fastened the guilt and inflicted the most exquisite tortures on a class hated for their abominations, called Christians by the populace …

Both St Peter and St Paul were to die in Rome, the centre of the civilized world in the first century AD. Both were martyred, according to the Christian tradition. While St Paul was beheaded, St Peter was crucified just as his mentor had been – but upside-down, it's said, at his own request. His death by crucifixion might have been ordered in sneering allusion to his Saviour's, but to St Peter it was an honour of which he was unworthy. Hence, the story has it, his desire to be executed the wrong way up. A great basilica was later raised up above his grave.

Fire and Sword

We view these events today as the beginnings of a great religious, historical and cultural tradition. For the Roman Empire, though, they were very much a minor, local thing. Most Romans were barely conscious of Christianity's existence. If they were, they saw it as the obscure offshoot of an obscure Middle-Eastern sect – one of innumerable little cults to be found in the most cosmopolitan city the world had ever seen. That it came to widespread attention at all was down to the opportunism of an Emperor in need of a convenient scapegoat for his political difficulties.

A wild paranoiac in the most powerful position in the world, Nero was a public menace, nothing less. His reign, which lasted from AD 54 till his deposition by a desperate Senate 14 years later, was characterized by

madness, murder and repression on a monstrous scale. Further disaster struck when fire ravaged Rome in AD 64. The impact of the conflagration was immense. According to the historian Tacitus, writing just a few years later:

'Rome, indeed, is divided into fourteen districts, four of which remained uninjured, three were levelled to the ground, while in the other seven were left only a few shattered, half-burnt relics of houses.'

Nero wasn't just the man in charge, it seems: some suggested that he had contrived the disaster deliberately, wishing to clear the site for a spectacular new palace he had in mind. As the Roman writer Suetonius says:

'… pretending to be disgusted with the old buildings, and the streets, he set the city on fire so openly, that many of consular rank caught his own household servants on their property with tow, and torches in their hands, but durst not meddle with them. There being near his Golden House some granaries, the site of which he exceedingly coveted, they were battered as if with machines of war, and set on fire, the walls being built of stone.'

In need of someone else to blame, writes Tacitus,

'Nero fastened the guilt and inflicted the most exquisite tortures on a class hated for their abominations, called Christians by the populace … Mockery of every sort was added to their deaths. Covered with the skins of beasts, they were torn by dogs and perished, or were nailed to crosses, or were doomed to the flames and burnt, to serve as a nightly illumination, when daylight had expired.'

This seems to have been the context in which, along with so many others, St Peter was arrested and put to death – just another minor move in the wider game of Roman politics.

Ups and Downs

The sense that it was a religion tried in the fire was to be central to the developing consciousness of Christianity, but it's clear that there was 'nothing personal' as far as Roman Emperors were concerned.

Opposite: St Stephen's ugly death – he was stoned by an angry mob (the young Saul – later St Paul – was a bystander) – takes on an extraordinary beauty in Pieter Paul Rubens' representation (c.1617). Its ability to transmute mortal pain into something more blessed was part of Christianity's appeal.

Nero's clampdown, horrifying as it may have been, was nakedly opportunistic. Time and time again through the second and third centuries, we find Christianity being attacked – or tolerated – with the same disregard. In between dreadful persecutions in the reigns of the Emperors Domitian, Trajan, Septimius Severus and Decius, came lengthy periods of easy-going acceptance: the mood typically turned ugly when economic times were hard.

Many priests and bishops were martyred in the reign of Valerian (253–60), including St Lawrence, reputedly burned on an iron grill. ('Turn me over, I'm done on this side…', he told his tormentors, tradition has it.) A few years later St Sebastian was forced to face a squad of archers. Such deaths were to take their

Opposite: St Paul was proud of being both a Jew and a Roman citizen: it is largely thanks to him that the Catholic Church was based in Rome. It was to his citizenship that he owed his good fortune in being beheaded – death by crucifixion was reserved for non-Romans.

Above: St Peter, it is said, on hearing that he was to be crucified, begged that he be hung up upside-down so as not to seem sacrilegiously to imitate his saviour. He was killed in Rome, and St Peter's Basilica built over his tomb.

places in a tradition of martyrology that was to be essential to the early Church's identity – like that of St Catherine of Alexandria, sentenced to have her body broken on a wagon wheel.

The Great Persecution

The Emperor Diocletian was tolerant by nature. By the end of the third century, however, the Empire was coming under strain. Financial mismanagement had resulted in economic difficulties in what was already so vast and unwieldy an Empire as to be effectively ungovernable – Diocletian had felt compelled to appoint four sub-emperors to reign across the regions on his behalf. It made sense at the same time to underline the 'Romanness' of the Roman world by

GETTING NERO'S NUMBER

DRIVEN UNDERGROUND BY Nero's persecution, the Christians had to communicate with one another secretly. Given that most shared Jewish backgrounds, they were familiar with the traditional numerology known as *gematria*. This ancient mystic system associated specific properties to different numbers in relation to the letters of the Hebrew alphabet.

Gematria was a vast and erudite subject in itself: you could spend a lifetime exploring its infinite subtleties. At its most basic level it offered a ready-made code for initiates. For the name Nero, the figures came to 666: notoriously, the 'Number of the Beast' in the Book of Revelation. For the early Christians, the Emperor was indeed the 'Antichrist'.

reaffirming its cultural values – none of course loomed larger than the old religion and its rituals.

In 303, therefore, the Emperor issued his 'Edict Against the Christians'. As the contemporary Christian scholar Eusebius put it, officials were 'to tear down the churches to their foundations and destroy the sacred scriptures by fire'. Those 'in honourable stations' were to be 'degraded' (reduced to slavery, in other words) if they refused to abjure their faith. Thus began the 'Great Persecution'. Contemporary sources claim that 10,000 martyrs were crucified side by side on the first day. And while this is surely an exaggeration, there's little doubt that many thousands must have died in a reign of religious terror that was to continue unabated for the next eight years.

'A Certain Religion of Lust'

These were dark times for the Church indeed. But there was no shortage of contemporary commentators ready to suggest that the Christians had brought their sufferings on themselves with dark deeds of their own.

It's a tribute to Jesus' radicalism that his central tenets seemed so hard for so many to take on board:

Below: Diocletian was responsible for the deaths of thousands in the 'Great Persecution' he launched in 303. Christians were tolerated for decades on end, but could never feel secure – in times of economic hardship they made the ideal scapegoats for all the Empire's ills.

'They love one another almost before they know one another', one scribe complained. Understandably, perhaps, Pagan contemporaries were cynical about the whole 'Love thy neighbour' message and found it hard to recognize the distinction being made between affectionate goodwill and sex. 'There is mingled among them a certain religion of lust', one said. 'They call one another promiscuously brothers and sisters'. The word 'promiscuously' here, of course, isn't used in a sexual sense, but it's easy to see how suspicious all this 'love' and siblinghood must have seemed. Suffice it to say that the suspicion of incest was never far away.

Feared and distrusted minority groups are just about invariably accused of sexual deviance, of course: 'Some say that they worship the genitals of their pontiff and priest', one critic said. The same source revealed: 'I hear that they adore the head of an ass, that basest

Above: 'The Christian Martyr's Last Prayer' was famously imagined by French artist Jean-Léon Gérôme in 1883. There's surprisingly little evidence for the tradition that Christians were 'thrown to the lions' in ancient Rome, but no doubt that in times of persecution many suffered torture and cruel death.

> I hear that they adore the head of an ass, that basest of creatures, consecrated by I know not what silly persuasion.

of creatures, consecrated by I know not what silly persuasion.' Such reports were – it goes without saying – entirely wild.

Worse than these absurd accusations, though, were the darker suspicions accruing around the Church, suspicions only encouraged by the desperate discretion of a beleaguered group. All too often down the ages, persecution has produced a vicious circle: an already mistrusted minority, in trying to lie low and avoid attention, creates an air of 'secrecy' and intensifies mistrust. The harder the Christians strove to avoid detection, the more feverish the speculation about their 'secret and nocturnal rites'. 'They know one another by secret signs and insignia', it was claimed.

Light in the Darkness

When the Roman persecutions were at their most intense, the Church was driven underground – quite literally: worship was conducted in the catacombs that lay beneath the streets of Rome.

As it happens, these catacombs had for the most part been constructed by the Christians themselves.

BLOOD SACRIFICE

THERE'S A WEARISOMELY familiar ring about some of the charges levelled at the early Christians, especially given that – to begin with, at any rate – they were mostly Jews. Around the end of the second century, the scholar Minucius Felix (himself a Christian) recorded some of the more lurid claims.

Of particular interest were the supposed 'initiation rites' of this evil creed. An infant having been concealed within a sack or pile of flour, the novice Christian was given a knife and told to stab the flour repeatedly, it was said, urged on by his sponsors to administer ever quicker and harder – although apparently harmless – blows. Only as the blood began to stain the flour did he realize that he had murdered an innocent young victim – but he'd join in the feast, bonding with his companions as they made their gory meal.

'Thirstily – O horror! – they lick up its blood; eagerly they divide its limbs. By this victim they are pledged together; with this consciousness of wickedness they are covenanted to mutual silence.'

If the story hazily recalls the idea of the Eucharist (the bread and wine becoming the body and blood of the crucified Christ), it also looks forward to one of the darkest Christian myths of medieval times. This attributed to Jews the custom of kidnapping and sacrificing Christian children so that their blood could be stirred into the mixture being prepared for their unleavened bread. The whole Jewish nation had to suffer the stigma of this 'Blood Libel' for centuries, and many Jews were to pay for such imaginary 'crimes' with their own lives.

Below: The ritual killing and bleeding of a Christian boy is essential to the celebration of the feast of Passover, as understood by the illustrator of the *Nuremberg Chronicle*, 1493. Anti-Semitism was an inseparable aspect of Catholicism in medieval times.

Above: Angelic reinforcements flock to Constantine's standard at the Battle of Milvian Bridge, on 28 October 312. The victorious ruler made Christianity the official religion of his Empire. An unusual take on the Gospel message, but Constantine's patronage transformed the fortunes of what was now the Church of Rome.

Where Pagan Romans had become happy to have their remains cremated, and just the ashes kept in an urn, they looked forward to the resurrection of the body – so, as far as was practicable, the body had to be kept intact. Hence the construction of these galleries, dug out of the soft and spongy volcanic tufa beneath the city: Christians came here to inter their dead and tend their tombs. Increasingly, though, as their troubles deepened, they came here to conduct their rites in secret: in some cases, icons were painted on the walls and impromptu churches took shape, deep underground.

Practical considerations may have brought them here – the catacombs offered the only obvious place of safety in a hostile city – but those who ventured down among the dead to pray for eternal life must surely have been fully conscious of the powerful symbolism too.

The thought of their forebears huddled here, praying to the Lord by flickering lamplight, has inspired Catholic believers ever since.

Unwilling Apostates

Not all were to prove as strong, of course. 'The spirit is willing but the flesh is weak,' as Jesus Christ observes in Matthew's Gospel. He himself was to ask (in the Garden of Gethsemane) that the cup of suffering should be taken from him. Even before the Passion proper, his right-hand-man St Peter had denied him

A DUBIOUS DONATION

CONSTANTINE WAS TO prove a generous and influential backer to his adoptive creed. He does *not*, however, appear to have issued that decree on the basis of which Pope Sylvester I and his successors asserted not just spiritual but temporal authority over the City of Rome and its environs (not to mention other lands scattered across Europe and North Africa). This so-called 'Donation of Constantine' justified the Church's worldly dominion over vast territories, and while many were to be lost over the centuries, the Popes held on to power in central Italy into modern times. Even today, the Vatican remains sovereign territory, its status sanctioned by custom, if not by legal title. In fact, the 'Donation of Constantine' was shown up as a forgery as early as 1440; it is thought to have been created in the eighth century.

three times. So it's hard to blame those believers who, in the face of daily harassment, torture and terror, ended up renouncing their Christian beliefs and at least going through the motions of resuming Pagan worship. Even so, those who held firm felt misgivings about the commitment of these *lapsi* (from the Latin for 'lapsed' or 'slipped') and acts of penitence were required before they were later readmitted to the Church.

A Place in the Sun

Diocletian died at the end of 311, by which time it was clear that his Great Persecution had failed – cruel and comprehensive as it had been. Many Christians were clearly continuing to worship in secret, while even those who had resumed the rites of the Pagan past had evidently done so only grudgingly out of fear. His successor in the east, Galerius, issued his own Edict of Toleration, ending the Persecution: the Empire stood to gain more by bringing the Christians back into the fold, he reasoned.

The Church was no longer illegal then, even if Christianity was still anything but mainstream. But things were now to move with bewildering speed. Challenging Galerius for rule over the Empire as a whole, his rival in the west, Constantius, died. His son Constantine asserted his claims over the entire Roman Empire. As the two Emperors and their armies

Opposite: No longer skulking in corners and catacombs, the Church was a great institution, its pontiff the equal of any worldly king. Sylvester I (represented here by Raphael) was said to have been offered Constantine's crown – but to have seen imperial power as superfluous to what he already had.

prepared to do battle by the Milvian Bridge, just north of Rome, Constantine underwent the most significant Christian conversion since St Paul.

A less spiritual character than Constantine it is difficult to imagine. Even so, like many a mystic before and since, he saw a vision. A good, old-fashioned Roman, true to traditional ways, he was a worshipper of *Sol Invictus* (the Unconquerable Sun). On the eve of the battle he looked up to see his blazing orb slowly sinking down the western sky. Suddenly, overlain across that burning disc, he saw the shape of a cross – and, beneath, an inscription: *In Hoc Signo Vinces* ('In this sign may you prevail'). Constantine embraced the new religion on the spot: having defeated Galerius he made Christianity the official religion of his Empire and the rest is ecclesiastical history.

Constantine's conversion could hardly have been more obviously opportunistic. Was this what Christ had meant when he warned: 'I bring not peace but the sword' (Matthew 10: 34)? Was this what Mary had meant in her Magnificat – 'He has toppled the mighty from their thrones' (Luke 1: 52)? Were God and Caesar really supposed to be quite so closely allied? After so many years of persecution, the leaders of the Church weren't in the mood to look a gift-horse in the mouth – the good that might be done in a Christian world was potentially limitless, after all. Despite this, some have inevitably felt that this was the first, fatal compromise by which the Church established its longstanding alliance with worldly authority, with privilege and power. At a stroke, Constantine had turned Christianity from a marginal cult into a great religion: Catholicism had triumphed – but had it also sold its soul?

II
GROWING PAINS

A minor cult had become the official religion of the Roman Empire, but success brought serious problems of its own. Soon, moreover, Arab armies would be building their own vast new Empire at bewildering speed, triumphing under the banner of Islam.

◆

'We are the times. Such as we are, such are the times.' — St Augustine

The meek, it seemed, had inherited the Earth: from persecuted sect to established religion, the Church's fortunes had been utterly transformed. Constantine's miracle-working touch had brought into being a great and powerful institution, the mighty Roman Empire's religious arm. Believers who had cowered in catacombs now gathered in great basilicas in the world's most important cities. Their clergy had the ear of the world's rulers.

Although Christianity's fortunes were now closely tied to the strength and power of the Roman Empire, this alliance was also a source of vulnerability. As of

Opposite: Roman power buckles before barbarian aggression: the Sack of Rome in 410 sent a shockwave through the entire ancient world. But Alaric and his Goths were just one threat to a Church which, having finally attained imperial acceptance, feared it might find itself as beleaguered as before.

AD 312, though, the potential pitfalls must have seemed extremely theoretical alongside the real and present benefits flowing from an association with the Roman state. In historical hindsight, it's clear that Constantine's own struggle to attain his throne (the fight which had in fact precipitated his Christian conversion) was a sign that all might not be well in the Empire. But this kind of 'trouble at the top' was by no means unprecedented in imperial Rome. It had never really affected the everyday administration of the Empire, nor obviously indicated any deeper instability in the state.

Barbarians at the Gate

As the fourth century went on, however, so did the divisions and the difficulties – even if the ship of state seemed able to weather any storm. The causes of the 'Decline and Fall' of the Roman Empire are notoriously elusive, of course: historians have blamed everything from imperial 'overstretch' to multiculturalism, from bureaucracy to sexual permissiveness. Christianity itself hasn't escaped censure, whether because its rise eroded the religious unity of the Empire or because its turn-the-other-cheek morality (supposedly) produced a generation unfit for soldiering.

The most obvious and immediate cause, however, was already unfolding far out on the Central Asian steppe, where the ferocious Huns – nomadic horsemen – were on the prowl. Pushing westward, they dislodged the people settled there, causing the irruption of the Visigoths into the Empire's eastern margins. The invaded now invaders, the Goths roamed and raided ever further westward until they defeated the Roman army at Adrianople in 378, killing the Emperor Valens.

A Tale of Two Cities

Still the pressure in the east continued. Further waves of barbarians spilled across into the Empire –

Below: Defeated at Adrianople, the wounded Emperor Valens rested up, but burned to death when unwitting Goths set the shelter he was hiding in on fire. So at least the story went: is this a hint that Christians were focusing more on the fiery sufferings awaiting sinners in the life beyond?

Opposite: The eyeglasses are anachronistic, but this study of St Augustine by the Master of Grossgmain (c. 1498) does suggest the colossal learning and uncompromising intellect of the man. Augustine's importance in the development of Catholic doctrine can't be overstated – nor, arguably, can the damage he has done.

the Germanic Alans and the Vandals and the Huns themselves. Again, the 'knock-on' effect was crucial: although a peace of sorts had been made with the Goths after Adrianople, in 410 they invaded Italy and laid siege to Rome. After months of slow starvation, the city yielded: in a spree of destruction the Goths sacked the Empire's capital.

If the human and material costs were cataclysmic, the symbolic damage was in some ways even worse: Rome's humiliation was just about complete. The Church was badly shaken too, its treasures plundered and its clergy killed – again, the psychological trauma was profound.

It seemed a whole civilization was at stake. St Augustine certainly saw the danger. It was in the aftermath of Rome's destruction that he started writing

Ource que lee deup citez
dont lune est de dieu et
lautre du diable sont par
uenues a leurs fins deues
par nre saueur Jhucrist
nous auons a disputer
diligement en ce liure
tant come nous pourrons
par lapde de dieu de quele condion soit le tourmet auc
mr au diable z a tous ceulx qui lui appartiennent.
Et ap mieulp ame a tenir ceste ordre a ce que apres
Je trutte de la beneurte des saints pour ce que le dit
tourment z beneurte puidurable sera auecques lee
corps. Et semble estre non crobable chose que lee corps

puissent pduer en tourmens que ceeulp demourer sas
aucune douleur en beneurte pardurable. et par ce qht
Je autap demonstre que joesse paine ne soit nue a no
auoire ce mandza monlt a demonstuer que on ope
plus legierement croire q limmortalite des corps sott
auenir aup saints aucune tristesse. De ceste ordre de
proceder ne sui point contre lee diuines escriptures
esquelee aucunesfois la beneurte des bons est mise
deuant. Si comme est ce on sest contenu q ceulx q
bien feront pront en la resurrection dole z ceulx qui
mal feront en la resurrection du jugement. mais y
est aucunesfois ordre contumete on contraux si com
me on sest escript. Le filz de femme enuoiera sec an
gres a ce quilz cueillent z amassent tous lee esclandes

his masterwork, *The City of God*. What the barbarians were to Rome, he reasoned, religious heretics were to the Church, whose spiritual integrity had to be secured at any cost.

The Price of Debate

Augustine, the Bishop of Hippo in what is now Algeria, knew all too well the risks of disunity. Across North Africa the Church was in real disarray. Since Christian worship had once been more allowed, a group known as 'Donatists' (after their movement's founder, Bishop Donatus Magnus) had been refusing to accept those members of the clergy who were seen to have

---

Hell, which is also called a lake of fire and brimstone, will be material fire, and will torment the bodies of the damned.

---

capitulated under the earlier persecution. The *Traditores*, or traitors – so-called because they had 'handed over' their holy books and trappings to the authorities when threatened – had formally been forgiven by the Church. But Donatus' followers, hardline perfectionists, saw their surrender as unpardonable: such apostates could have no place in the true Church. The result had been that two supposedly Catholic churches had been co-existing rancorously side by side – it simply wasn't sustainable, Augustine thought.

Looking beyond his own diocese to the wider Church, Augustine could see other forces for disunity: there were the Arians (followers of Arius), who disputed the doctrine of the Trinity, arguing that, as the 'Son of God', Christ was a separate entity from his Father. Another group, following Pelagius, believed that Adam's Sin hadn't of itself been finally damning for the individual soul: if you conducted yourself well enough in life, you could save yourself without the necessity of God's help. Today, in a secular age, such disputes may seem nit-pickingly petty, but theologically

Opposite: Dunked by demons in pools of fire, souls suffer an eternity of torment: this picture of Hell comes, fittingly, from a French edition of *De Civitate Dei* ('The City of God'). It was here that St Augustine sketched out the sort of punishments awaiting the unrepentant sinner.

the disagreements were profound. More to the point, in practical terms, Augustine's concerns were understandable: these differences had the potential to tear the Church of Christ apart.

A Punitive Faith

Augustine was humane by nature, but his fears for the Church seem to have driven him to fanaticism. In reaction to Pelagius' optimism, he offered a brutally pessimistic survey of the human spiritual condition. Not only was he the first to formulate the central doctrine of 'Original Sin', he did more than anyone else to shape the idea of hell.

While warning of the 'wages of sin', the scriptures had been surprisingly vague about what these might be beyond a few poetic hints about 'pools of fire' and banishment to the 'outer darkness'. Augustine spelled things out more clearly – there was no room for misunderstanding his assertion that:

'Hell, which is also called a lake of fire and brimstone, will be material fire, and will torment the bodies of the damned.'

By 'material fire', of course, Augustine meant real, flaming fire that literally burned the body's physical flesh – it was anything but metaphorical, in other words.

Here began what for many modern theologians was an unwarranted – and even un-Christian – obsession with the intimate details of damnation and a sadistic interest in the terrible topography of hell. And, in Augustine's doctrine of 'Original Sin', a profoundly internalized self-hatred extended into every corner of the Catholic's emotional and sexual life. Only in very recent times has the Church begun to allow its adherents to make some sort of peace with themselves psychologically, and started to shake off one of the very darkest aspects of its history.

A Rival Religion

Augustine's vision of Catholicism as a city under siege was frighteningly convincing but perhaps unduly pessimistic: the Church was to survive – however uncomfortably – the Fall of Rome. The barbarians who in 476 deposed the unfortunate boy-Emperor Romulus Augustulus were at the very least loosely allied with the Christian cause.

Within just over a century, however, a still more serious threat to the Church would arise 2000 miles to the east in Arabia. Muhammad's first divine

'JUST PERSECUTION'

In his rage for orthodoxy, Augustine eventually came to feel that there was a place for the punishment of heretics not only in the afterlife but in this life, by officials of the Church.

Having earlier spoken out against torture as an instrument of oppression, he later started to distinguish between the persecutions of the old Pagan state and that 'just persecution which the Church of Christ inflicts upon the wicked'. Citing the example of St Paul, he pointed out that his being struck down by violent force on the Road to Damascus had enabled him to find a truer faith founded in doctrine and in love:

'It is wonderful how he who entered the gospel in the first instance under the compulsion of bodily punishment, afterwards laboured more in the gospel than all they who were called by word only; and he who was compelled by the greater influence of fear to love, displayed that perfect love which casts out fear.'

'Why, therefore,' Augustine asked, 'should not the Church use force in compelling her lost sons to return?' Tragically, he asked the question rhetorically.

---

visions date from AD 610. At the time a middle-aged businessman in Mecca, the Prophet received a series of visits from the Archangel Gabriel who dictated to him the word of *Allah* – God. A new religion was brought into being: *Islam* – the name meant 'submission', in the sense of yielding to the divine will. Like Judaism and Christianity (for whose scriptures and traditions Muhammad had much respect) it was a monotheism – recognizing only a single deity. As such, inevitably, it affronted the Pagan beliefs of the Arabs at large, and life became uncomfortable for Muhammad and his handful of converts who came into conflict with the *Quraysh*, Mecca's wealthy elite. In 622 the Muslims left for the neighbouring city of Medina. Relations with the city's three tribes of Jews were good, at least to begin with. As hostilities with Mecca continued, though, suspicions between the two groups grew, Muhammad and his followers fearing that the Jews might make alliance with their Arab enemies.

Holy War

In time the Muslims prevailed, though, and their victory marked the start of one of the most astonishing campaigns of conquest the world has ever seen. By the time the Prophet died in 632, to be succeeded by his father-in-law, the first Caliph Abu Bakhr, the Arabs had already carried the word by force of arms – and inspiration – through much of the Middle East.

Although their warlike nature had always been recognized, the Arabs had hitherto been dismissed as raiders, a mere nuisance: now, however, their aggression was channelled by a passionate faith. Christianity was in retreat, with the destruction of three of Catholicism's five patriarchal sees: Jerusalem, Antioch (Syria) and Alexandria, in Egypt. Across North Africa – the Maghreb – they continued: any dissensions among Augustine's spiritual descendants were rendered academic as the forces of Islam spilled across the region in an advancing tide.

In the early years of the eighth century, Arab armies pushed west from Libya across the entire length of the Maghreb. In the east, in 717–18 a determined siege of Constantinople was successfully resisted, but no one was under any illusion that Europe was safe from Islamic conquest. By this time Spain was already largely under Muslim occupation. The first raiding party of Arabs and Islamicized Berbers had crossed the Straits of Gibraltar in 711: Tariq ibn-Ziyad's warriors crushed the defenders sent against them. By 718, Iberia's Catholic Visigoth rulers had been defeated by these 'Moors' and almost the entire peninsula was under Islamic rule. Only in the far north, in Asturias, did the Muslims suffer a setback: in these mountains, a little pocket of Christendom remained.

Turned at Tours

On into France they advanced: this time, though, the Catholic Princes managed to come together to repel the invaders. In 732, at the Battle of Tours, near Poitiers, under the command of Charles Martel

('Charles the Hammer'), 30,000 Franks lined up to face a force of 80,000 Muslim men. The Moorish cavalry came at them in waves but, a Christian witness reports, the Franks stood firm, 'as motionless as a wall'. Their shields locked together, all in line, they presented a seamless barrier, 'like a belt of ice frozen solid, and not to be dissolved'.

In the decades and centuries that followed, the Muslims were pushed slowly southward, although their kingdom of al-Andalus still covered most of Spain and Portugal. Only in the second millennium was it to be confined to that southern region, which is still known

Below: On the side of the angels now, the Visigoths had established a Catholic kingdom in Iberia. In the early eighth century, however, it was overrun by Islamic invaders from North Africa. Here King Roderic is killed in single combat by Tariq ibn-Zayid at Guadalete, 711.

as Andalucía. The Caliphs of the Umayyad dynasty had made it their base, holing up here after the rest of the Empire fell under Abbasid rule in 750, their capital at Córdoba a match even for Baghdad in its astonishing mosques and palaces, its gardens, its crafts, its culture and its learning.

Back to the Margins

It was an age of magnificence, of creativity and – for the most part – tolerance. There had been – and would in the future be – many much darker times for the Catholic Church. The Caliphs were easy-going about the presence of the *dhimmi* – the community of non-believers, such as Christians and Jews – in their midst. There's an element of wishful thinking in the recently-fashionable suggestion that al-Andalus was some sort of multicultural utopia: the Islamic rulers seem to

Opposite: Charles Martel stems the advancing Muslim tide at the Battle of Tours, an epic victory for the armies of Christian Europe. Not only did the Frankish triumph mark the deliverance of France, it was the first indication that Islamic power could suffer significant defeat.

have disdained the Christians' creed and milked them cynically for tax. In the annals of persecution, though, such low-level harassment scarcely registers: Catholics had little to complain of in Islamic Spain.

The real offence was to Christian self-esteem. The Church and Christendom seemed completely to have lost the initiative: they were on the defensive, responding to events. As the Muslims made strides in science, philosophy, art and literature, moreover, Christian culture was coming to seem backward, crude: who had the 'civilization' and who were the 'barbarians' now? What had appeared to be the religion of the future had been brushed aside, apparently without effort, over much of its territory and there was little confidence that further advances could be resisted. Christ had promised eternal life, but could his Church really deliver? Had history already passed it by?

ROMAN RAMPAGE

THE DESERT-DWELLING ARABS were traditionally known as fighters on dry land, but they'd established an important tradition of seafaring as well. Arab vessels carried trade goods – and the Islamic word – from the Red Sea and the Gulf down much of the eastern side of Africa; Arab raiders attacked Christian centres in the Mediterranean. In the early eighth century, they established an important base at Messina, Sicily, from where further attacks were mounted around the coasts of southern Italy. In 846, helpless defenders looked on as Arab raiders rampaged through Rome and the Vatican: even St Peter's Basilica was not spared.

Chaos ensued when, in 846, Arab attackers raided Rome, burning and looting in the very sanctuary of the Catholic faith. The confrontation between Christianity and Islam was to shape the history of both great religions over the next few centuries.

III

SACRED SLAUGHTER: THE CRUSADES

Massacre thy neighbour? The medieval Church had a strange way of showing Christian love. Muslims, Jews and 'heretics' were all on the receiving end as clerics and kings shored up their authority and power by orchestrating attacks on other groups.

◆

'He that doth not take up his cross and follow me is unworthy of me.'

'Deus vult!' – 'God wills it!' – came the cry from the crowd as Pope Urban II made his heartfelt call to Christian arms. What God willed, it seemed, was that they march off to the Middle East and make war with the Muslims there. The Church's claim to comprehend the will of God was to inspire a long and bloody series of atrocities from the end of the eleventh century through to the fourteenth. Urban's speech was certainly arresting. The Saracens, he said, his voice trembling with emotion, had been

'penetrating deeper and deeper into Christian lands' to Europe's east. They had defeated the Christians seven times in battle, had 'killed or taken prisoner a great many, destroyed fine churches and laid waste to extensive areas of land.' Having captured Anatolia, they had pitched their camp on the banks of the Bosporus – on the very threshold of Christian Europe, in other words. Scarcely able to continue with his peroration, apparently on the point of breaking down completely, he pleaded with those clerics, knights and nobles who had gathered at the Council of Clermont for their support.

The Red Cross
'This is why I beg you and urge you – no, not just I: the Lord Himself begs and implores you, as heralds of Christ, whether poor or wealthy, to rush off and expel this rabble from your brothers' territories, and to bring rapid relief to those who worship Christ.'

Opposite: Urban II, caller of the First Crusade, seems to have envisaged only a very limited local action to assist the eastern churches. In the event, the campaign he set in motion was to catch the imagination of western Europe, dominating religion and politics for several centuries.

First prostrating themselves on the floor before the papal throne, they rose and went spilling out on to the streets in a shouting, cheering throng. To the outside observer, they may have looked no more than a well-dressed mob: they themselves, though, felt seized with sacred emotion. Enlisted by their Pope in what amounted to a militarized pilgrimage, they pinned on their clothes a red fabric cross – in French, *croisade*.

The Holy City

Pope Urban II's summons, in 1095, came in response to a request from the Byzantine Emperor, Alexius I. Informing His Holiness of the invasion of Asia Minor by the Seljuk Turks, he requested his help in defending Christian Constantinople. At this stage, neither Alexius nor Urban envisaged anything more than a small

---

> This is why I beg you and urge you ... whether poor or wealthy, to rush off and expel this rabble from your brothers' territories ...

French force to be sent in support of Constantinople's defenders, under Byzantine leadership. But Constantinople, with all its glories, did not haunt the Western imagination the way Jerusalem did: medieval maps often placed Jesus' city at the centre of the world. The streets along which Christ had walked, the scenes of his passion and death – Jerusalem was a uniquely special city. The thought of a pilgrimage here had inspired Christians for generations. A surprising number of people had indeed made the journey to see the land they'd read about in scripture or been told of in church – an undertaking which could take them many years.

They'd succeeded in doing so despite the fact that, for some four centuries, these 'Holy Places' had been held by Muslims: they'd been fleeced by traders and tax-gatherers and pushed around by officials, but never seriously abused. Still less had they been prevented from pursuing a pilgrimage that the Muslims looked on more with mild amusement than hostility. Now, however, all of a sudden Western rulers decided to feel outraged: how could Christianity's holiest shrines not be in Christian hands?

Fighting for Salvation

Those who answered Urban's summons, he subsequently clarified, would automatically receive an 'indulgence' – time off from the years of suffering they might otherwise expect in purgatory when they died. Some modern historians have attributed mercenary motives to the Crusaders, arguing that they marched eastward only in search of power and plunder. They have underestimated the part played by the fear of death – and, more particularly, of damnation – in the medieval mind. There was nothing fake about the fervour the Crusade evoked, although arguably much of that was superficial – even cynical – to the extent that a sort of spiritual self-interest appears to have prevailed.

It took Europe's kings a year to mobilize for the First Crusade: ordinary people were a great deal quicker off the mark. Within weeks of Urban's appeal, a rag-tag army of beggars, peasants, artisans and lowly knights was already on the march. Women and children flocked along on this great adventure. Most came from southern Germany and Northern France. There, itinerant preachers were whipping up a fever of expectation that the end of the world was coming, and that people should secure their salvation in a final battle with Satan and his Pagan forces. The most famous of these preachers, Peter the Hermit, roamed the towns and cities of France and Flanders, calling all to join what was to become known as the People's Crusade, and he marshalled many thousands in that cause.

The People's Pogrom

Impatient with a history of kings and queens, modern historians have inevitably been drawn to the story of the People's Crusade – aptly named, for it was truly a democratic phenomenon. For better and for worse the poor of medieval Europe appear to have been every bit as capable of cruelty and greed as their betters. The Crusade was wildly anarchic in its organization (if it can even be called that) and utterly undiscriminating in its violence.

Muslims or Jews, what was the difference? Why travel hundreds of miles to face an unknown and

Opposite: The Council of Clermont, 1095, became a rallying point for a western Christendom which saw itself as being threatened by the Islamic danger from the east. Pope Urban's impassioned speech moved all who heard it – and echoed across Europe – soon great armies were marching in a military pilgrimage for Christ.

et aultres sains lieux la enuiron.
Et les ypiens pbibitans z demou
rans . z que les aultres par eulx
tyranniquement z Jnhumame
ment tues . Ils auoient resemi
en Jnfelicieuse bie a fyn que sur
eulx en lopzobze du saint nom
ypien prissent continuer plus
longuement leurs Jnsatiables

aultés . Et comment Ils
les tenoient en tzip opzobzieuse
captiuite z seruiaise . ou tresgrant
deshonneur z opzobze de tous
les ypiens . Concluant z mon
strant par diuerses raisons tres
euidentes que le saint peuple
ypien ne debuoit plus souffen
nendurer que ses sains lieux vet

KILLERS OF CHRIST

THE CONCEPT OF 'race' is a comparatively recent one, a product (ironically) of the 'Enlightenment' that transformed the fields of philosophy and science from the seventeenth century. It's accordingly anachronistic to talk of 'racism' in the pre-modern period. That doesn't of course mean that equality and easy-going tolerance reigned, just that prejudices were articulated and justified differently.

Hatred of the Jews in medieval Europe was virulent: they were despised and feared by the wider populace for their supposed role in killing Christ. Their economic function in an age before banking was also profoundly unpopular – even as it was obviously necessary. The lending of money at interest was banned by the Church, who saw it as amounting to the buying and selling of time – God's property, not a commodity in which mortal men had any business trading.

Then, as in so many centuries since, the Jews were the scapegoat of first resort in Christian communities when crops failed, plague struck or times were otherwise hard. The greater the persecution, the more marginalized the Jews became, the more unknowable and 'alien' they came to seem – and the deeper the fear and suspicion with which they were viewed.

Anti-Semitism was by no means confined to the lower orders: Godfrey de Bouillon, leader of the French in the 'official' First Crusade, vowed at one point that he wouldn't even begin his journey to the Holy Land till he'd 'avenged the blood of the crucified one with Jewish blood' and completely destroyed anybody who 'bore the name of Jew'.

Left: The noble crusader of nineteenth-century stereotype gave way in modern times to a more cynically-imagined opportunist, bent on plunder. Neither image is adequate: the Crusaders seem to have been swept up in something real – a rush of sincere (if borderline-hysterical) piety.

frightening foe when Christ's killers were to be found in the ghettoes here at home? More and more people travelled through Lorraine towards the Rhine – in almost the opposite direction from Jerusalem. There they forced their way into the cities of Aachen and Cologne, where local hooligans were emboldened to attack those who, not content with crucifying Our Blessed Saviour, now tortured honest Christian men with the usurious interest on their loans.

'This slaughter of Jews was done first by citizens of Cologne,' a Christian eyewitness, Albert of Aix, reports:

'These suddenly fell upon a small band of Jews and severely wounded and killed many; they destroyed the houses and synagogues of the Jews and divided among themselves a very large amount of money. When the Jews saw this cruelty, about two hundred in the silence of the night began flight by boat to Neuss. The pilgrims and crusaders discovered them, and after taking away

all their possessions, inflicted on them similar slaughter, leaving not even one alive.'

Further massacres and attacks on synagogues took place in Speyer and Mainz. In the latter, seeing the cruel ferocity with which the Christians were attacking their neighbours, Jewish men murdered their wives, and mothers killed their children, as an act of mercy.

No mercy was shown in the town of Worms. Here over 800 Jews were murdered in response, it appears, to a rumour that some of their co-religionists had murdered a Christian man and thrown his body down a well. Allowing him to rot down there a while, they had then tried to use the contaminated water to poison the supply of the city as a whole. Many Jews, fleeing the fury of the mob, had sought sanctuary with the local bishop in his palace. Unimpressed by his ecclesiastical authority, the 'Crusaders' simply smashed down the gates, stormed in and massacred those they discovered hiding.

Mayhem on the March

At last, the Crusade began making its way southeastward, out of French and German lands. Robbing, murdering and raping as they went, they moved on through Hungary and the Balkans: Alexius I was appalled at the ragged, hungry shower that turned up outside the walls of Constantinople in the summer of 1096. Rather than have them admitted – even for a moment – into his city, he had these motley 'Crusaders' shipped across the Bosporus to Asia Minor without

further ado. There they were simply swatted aside by the army of the Seljuk ruler, Kilij Arslan. They had come an awfully long way for such an ignominious defeat.

The First Crusade proper got off to a more promising start. The Crusaders quickly captured the Seljuk capital, Nicaea, in what is now northwestern Turkey. But as they fought their way over the Anatolian mountains into northern Syria, triumph turned inexorably into disaster. Despite the months of preparation that had gone before, serious logistical

BLESSED BEASTS

THE MORE SOBER Christian commentators viewed the 'People's Crusade' askance, to put it mildly. Albert of Aix was completely horrified. This distinguished chronicler did all he could to distance himself (and his faith) from what he seems to have seen as a hideously parodic pilgrimage, a savage satire on human stupidity and greed.

The 'Crusaders', he claimed, 'asserted that a certain goose was inspired by the Holy Spirit, and that a she goat was not less filled by the same Spirit. These they made their guides on this holy journey to Jerusalem. They worshipped these animals excessively; and most of the people following them – like beasts themselves – believed with their whole minds that this was the true course. May the hearts of the faithful be free from the thought that the Lord Jesus wished the Sepulchre of His most sacred body to be visited by brutish and insensate animals, or that He wished these to become the guides of Christian souls, which by the price of His own blood He deigned to redeem from the filth of idols!'

Yet such critiques ring hollow given the bestial cruelty of the First Crusade as it unfolded the following year: would 'Lord Jesus' have found the attitudes and conduct of his 'noble' followers so much more appealing?

inadequacies became apparent: thousands died during the relatively short – but desperately demanding – march to Palestine. A vast army – not just men (and women and children) but horses and beasts of burden – had to make their way across arid terrain in a time of scorching heat. Feeding and, especially, watering them all was an impossibility. Many thousands expired in agony: of the 100,000 who had set out, only 40,000 arrived exhausted at the gates of Antioch.

The Agony of Antioch

As became the strategic centre of Syria, the city was heavily fortified: undaunted, the Crusaders settled down for a lengthy siege. Beset by hunger, and harried by fighters foraying out from the city in nighttime raids, the Christians had an extremely unpleasant time. One in seven died of starvation, Matthew of Edessa reports (the figure was almost certainly much higher among the common soldiery). After seven long, hard months, Bohemund of Tarent talked the city's Christian inhabitants into betraying their fellow-citizens and opening the gates. On 3 June 1098, Antioch was taken and thousands of its inhabitants were slaughtered. They included a great many Christians, but the Crusaders didn't distinguish, falling on all in a vengeful rage.

... Even Dogs

Buoyed up by this success, the Crusaders were able to hold their prize against a Turkish relief force led by Kerbogha of Mosul. Mopping up resistance in the area around, they attacked the city of Ma'ara. They were winning their war, it seemed, but they were no

> ... to relate that many on our side, driven mad by the pains of starvation, cut chunks of meat from the buttocks of Saracen corpses they found in the field.

nearer to being able to feed themselves: both sides lacked supplies after so many months of fighting back and forth. At Ma'ara, it was claimed, the Crusaders fell upon the vanquished defenders and the terrified citizenry and – not content with killing them – tore at their bodies for flesh to eat.

Truth is the first casualty in war, it is said, and horror-stories are never lacking when there's an enemy to be smeared, but the reports of cannibalism at Ma'ara

Opposite: The Crusaders took their first great prize, the Syrian city of Antioch, in the June of 1098. Starting as it seemed they meant to go on, they fell upon a defenceless populace in a vengeful rage. Thousands were slaughtered in the bloodletting – including Christians.

don't come mainly from Muslim sources. Rather, it was in the testimony of shocked Christian chroniclers like Radulph of Caen that those at home read of children roasted over fires on spits and adults being boiled in macabre stews. 'I shudder', wrote Fulcher of Chartres, 'to relate that many on our side, driven mad by the pains of starvation, cut chunks of meat from the buttocks of Saracen corpses they found in the field. Having set out to cook them over their fires, they couldn't even wait till they were properly done, but fell upon them, gorging like wild beasts.'

Albert of Aix confirmed the incident, although his report is as remarkable for the sliding scale of atrocity he seems to see in the fact that the Crusaders 'didn't just eat Turks and Saracens but even dogs'. Their army now numbering only 20,000, the Crusaders advanced

Below: A French tapestry of the seventeenth century shows the heroic light in which the capture of Jerusalem (1099) was later to be cast. The reality was a senseless spree of killing, the Crusaders killing Muslims, Jews – and Christians – alike; 'neither women nor children were spared,' one chronicler recorded.

Opposite: Bernard of Clairvaux proclaimed the Second Crusade at the request of Pope Eugene III, calling kings and commoners alike to the red-cross banner. St Bernard seems to have been horrified when he saw the anarchy he had unleashed, personally intervening to try to prevent several German pogroms.

on Jerusalem, arriving outside its gates on 7 June 1099. After another siege, a party led by Godfrey of Bouillon breached the walls on 13 July. They celebrated with a spree of killing. 'No one had ever heard of such a bloodbath among Pagan peoples as this one,' wrote Archbishop William of Tyre. Thousands of men, women and children were put to the sword: no distinction was made between Muslims and Jews. 'If you had been there,' wrote Fulcher of Chartres, 'you would have seen our feet stained to our ankles in the blood of the slain … none of them was left alive; neither women nor children were spared.'

Diminishing Returns

It would be an exaggeration to say that it was all for nothing. Four 'Crusader States' were established

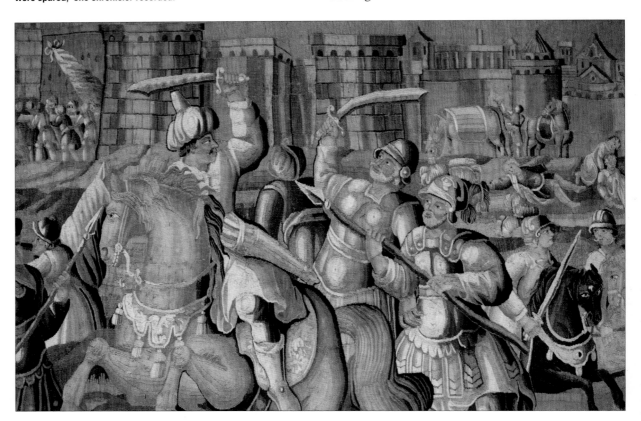

in the Middle East: the Kingdom of Jerusalem, the Principality of Antioch and the Counties of Edessa and Tripoli (in northern Lebanon) became important centres for commercial and cultural commerce between East and West. From the modern perspective, it's tempting to see these states as what we would call 'colonies'. Except that the overwhelming superiority in wealth, technology and military strength the European powers were to enjoy over their subject nations in the nineteenth century was to be entirely absent here. If anything, it was the other way round. By the standards of an Islamic world that was way ahead in science and learning, the 'Franks' really were the rude 'barbarians' the Muslims saw them as. They were easily to be dislodged by a united and organized Islamic force. In 1144 Imad ad-Din Zengi reconquered Edessa, in northern Syria, with his Seljuk army, prompting alarm in Europe and an unsuccessful Second Crusade (1145–49).

The First Crusade had established a depressing template: the Crusaders proved more adept at massacring Jews in Germany during their muster for the wars than they were at dealing with well-armed and well-commanded Muslim armies. Again, the ghettoes of Cologne, Mainz, Speyer and Worms were to bear the brunt. The campaign in the Middle East was ineffective. It was only thanks to continuing disunity among the Muslims that the Crusaders were able to maintain some sort of hold in the Holy Land. When the Muslims found a strong and capable leader in the shape of Salah ad-Din ('Saladin', as the westerners called him), they retook Jerusalem easily in 1187.

The Brutality of Richard I

For all the chivalric myths about Richard the Lionheart the Third Crusade he led was, at very best, a qualified success. Except in atrocity, where it was well up to the mark. An old-fashioned English historiography rooted in public-school values of sportsmanship and fair play has bequeathed to us an idealized view of the relationship between England's Richard I and Saladin – one of elaborate courtesy based on mutual respect.

Left: The Second Crusade (1145) began with this solemn scene in the Basilica of Saint-Denis (now in northern Paris), Louis VII vowing to fight for Christ. Subsequent events proved anticlimactic: both French and German contingents were ignominiously defeated, the Holy Places left more firmly than ever in Muslim hands.

In fact, relations between them were ill-tempered and vindictive. Having taken the Syrian city of Acre in 1191, Richard opened negotiations by having 2700 Muslim prisoners put to death. Saladin responded with mass-executions of Christian captives. By 1192, the Crusade had secured visiting rights for Christian pilgrims, but nothing else. The Holy City certainly lay more firmly than ever in Muslim hands.

Sack and Sacrilege

Would it be fourth time lucky? It depends upon your point of view. The Crusaders of 1202–04 did return home as conquerors. Not of Jerusalem, though, but of Constantinople, a Christian city. Short of money, the force sent out by Pope Innocent III diverted to the Byzantine capital to shake down the Emperor Alexius III for funds. Finding him uncooperative, they ended up laying a long and cruel siege.

Crusading on the Home Front

The whole crusading ideal was looking a little tarnished by now, it might be thought, but that didn't stop churchmen and rulers from devising ever more 'Crusades'. In Iberia, the centuries-long drive to take back Spain and Portugal from the 'Saracens' came to be seen as not just a campaign of conquest but a holy war. And then, in 1209, crusading came home with a vengeance to the south of France, when Pope Innocent III proclaimed a war against the Cathars.

Opposite: Waylaid by Mesud I's Seljuk Turks, the German crusading army was defeated at Dorylaeum in 1147. King Conrad III escaped with a handful of survivors, but they could do little to help a French force which was to be badly mauled itself at Damascus the following year.

Below: Salah ad-Din Yusuf ibn Ayyub, or 'Saladin', a warrior of Kurdish birth, led Islamic forces with daring and with flair. Despite the 'Lionhearted' courage of England's Richard I, the Third Crusade was another failure, Saladin strengthening his hold on the 'Holy Places'.

These simple, largely uneducated and yet earnestly idealistic men and women had never done anybody any harm – paradoxically, this very innocence increased the threat they posed. The greed and cynicism of the Church was particularly apparent to the poorest in society: like many others the length and breadth of Europe, those of southern France felt they had seen through the hypocrisy of those who were supposed to be their spiritual guides. Unlike disillusioned souls elsewhere, though, they had found comfort in another creed.

Catharism conceived of the cosmos as essentially dualistic, a system in which God and Satan warred with one another and body and soul were locked in eternal opposition. The soul was eternal and belonged in heaven, the realm of God and of light. All that was material and mortal belonged to this world – that of Satan – and was dark and bad. Since Christ, according to the scriptures, was 'the Word made flesh', it followed that he and his teachings must be evil too. The worldliness of the Church was all too obvious. Far from being the 'Bride of Christ', preached Cathar Arnald Hot, it was 'espoused of the Devil and its doctrine diabolical'. Such teachings drew on a deep well of frustrated idealism, and many flocked to follow what seemed to be a purer path. King Philippe II was concerned at what he saw as a threat to the social order. As far as Pope Innocent III was concerned, Catharism could not be ignored. The heretics were like

Above: In the killing fields of Languedoc, poor peasant families were slaughtered in their thousands, but towns like Béziers certainly weren't spared. Anything up to 20,000 may have been killed here; afterwards, in the words of the Pope's legate Arnaud Amalric, 'the whole city was despoiled and burned'.

Opposite: 'Our men spared no one,' crowed papal legate Arnaud Amalric after the taking of Béziers in 1209. Many good Catholics must have been in the southern French city along with the Cathar 'heretics'. 'Never mind. Kill them all, and let God sort them out,' Abbot Amalric said.

the 'Saracens', he said, and in 1209 he proclaimed a crusade against this enemy within.

Massacred in God's Name

From the military point of view, the 'Albigensian Crusade' was a grotesquely one-sided affair: it took its name from the town of Albi, a hotbed of heresy. Although local magnates like Count Raymond of Toulouse were involved (covetousness of his lands and power was an unacknowledged cause of the Crusade, as far as the northern French barons were concerned), for the most part the 'enemy' were defenceless peasants. All the panoply of medieval war-making – mounted knights with retinues of foot soldiers, including archers and crossbowmen, as well as companies of mercenaries – were deployed against unarmed civilians. Siege-engines smashed through the walls of country towns.

les habitants de
Beziers furent
mis a mort les

protéger de la mort
ni eroix, ni autel, ni
erucifix! les misé .

No mercy was shown towards the defeated – the crushing of heresy was sacred work. At Béziers, the Papal Legate boasted, 20,000 men, women and children were put to the sword. Over a thousand were burned alive after seeking sanctuary inside a church. Although Pope Innocent tried to rein in the carnage from about 1213, it had acquired an unstoppable momentum. All told, as many as a million may have died.

Foreshadowing the Yellow Star

Elsewhere in western Europe, Catharism had never gained ground the way it had in France's Languedoc

Below: Innocent III proclaimed a Fifth Crusade in 1215 at the same Lateran Council at which he announced his hostile measures against the Jews.

– but there were was always that old, reliable scapegoat-group, the Jews. Hostility towards 'Christ's Killers' had never entirely gone away but it had flared up recurrently in times of economic and social stress. In York, in 1190, for instance, word of a pogrom prompted local Jews to seek refuge in the tower of the city's castle. Anti-Semitic feeling had been whipped up by Richard Mabelys and other nobles who seem to have been motivated mainly by the consciousness that they owed large sums of money to the Jews and didn't want to pay it back. But the Church's representatives were ready and willing to cast a cloak of piety over this persecution: while the Jews cowered inside the tower, a priest celebrated mass outside and urged on his congregants against the Jews. So it continued for six days, at which point their despairing captives – fearing

BLOOD LIBEL

THE JEWS, RATHER than the Romans, had always borne the blame as the killers of Christ: a grim mythology had grown up around this 'fact'. In 1144, rumours erupted in Norwich, England, that a little boy named William who had gone missing had been abducted and ritually crucified by the city's Jews. Drawing off young William's blood, they had mixed this in with meal to make their *matzos*, or unleavened bread. The story was taken up internationally, sparking off a wave of persecution, with similar kidnappings and killings reported across much of Europe. This despite the strict prohibition on the eating of blood-derivatives insisted on by the Jewish Torah – and the expansion of the original story in an investigation ordered by Pope Innocent IV in 1247.

The Church's own ambivalence can't have helped: although investigation after investigation formally refuted the 'Blood Libel' officially, priests at local level shared the prejudices of the masses. And the cult of 'Saint William of Norwich' received at least tacit recognition from the Church after a series of miraculous cures were allegedly worked at the supposed 'martyr's' shrine. When, in 1255, the body of a nine-year-old boy was found at the bottom of a well in Lincoln, he too was said to have been ritually murdered. Again, the 'Blood Libel' was repeated and again attacks on Jewish communities in Lincoln and abroad were unleashed. And again, the Church was ambivalent in its reaction. On the one hand, officially, it scoffed at the stories and deprecated the attacks on Jews; on the other, it was only too happy to recognize the miracles that were supposedly worked by 'Little St Hugh of Lincoln' and cash in on the pious pilgrims who flocked from far and wide to see his shrine.

death or, still worse, forced baptism – committed collective suicide: 150 died.

In 1215, anti-Semitism was given the official imprimatur of the Catholic Church, whose Fourth Lateran Council issued a series of decrees against the Jews. To begin with, Jews were prohibited from employing Christians as servants – no Jew should have authority over any Christian, in other words. Notoriously, it further stipulated that Jews (and Muslims) had to wear distinctive garb so that their 'perfidious' presence should always be evident to the Christian communities among which they lived. The brutal enforcement of Catholic orthodoxy in the reconquered kingdoms of Spain had forced loyal Jews and Muslims underground, giving rise to a whole new bogeyman: that of the sinisterly secretive crypto-alien, preying on innocent Christians. It was an aspect of the Jews' malicious cunning that they could conceal

Right: Desperate Jews in York in 1190 were reduced to killing themselves, their wives and families to pre-empt the threat of murder or forced conversion. Never exactly in short supply, Christian hypocrisy reached special depths in the hatred felt for Jewish 'usurers' on whose services so many relied.

themselves in plain sight. The Lateran Council's orders were supposed to drive this hidden menace out into the open – there should be no way for the Jews to conceal their secret 'shame'.

The Northern Crusades

The Christians of medieval Europe knew (or thought they did) about the Jews from their sacred scriptures. By and large, though, they had only the vaguest idea of what Islam was. In records of the fighting in Iberia and the Middle East, the enemy is generally referred to in ethnic terms as 'Saracens' or 'Moors'. Where their beliefs are concerned, they tend to be described as

Below: Overlooking Latvia's Gauja Valley, Sigulda Castle was built by the Brothers of the Sword in the thirteenth century. As their name suggests, the Brothers had a rough and ready way of making converts. (They were later absorbed into the Order of Teutonic Knights.)

'Pagans'. In truth, of course, Islam is one of the three 'Religions of the Book', sharing the Old Testament both with Judaism and Christianity. All three faiths revere Abraham as a founding patriarch and prophet; all share fundamental values and beliefs.

In Christian Europe's remoter northern fringes, however, real 'Pagans' did still exist. Around the Baltic, in Lithuania, Latvia and northern Prussia, people still followed age-old religious practices, worshipping the deities they saw in the sun, moon and stars, and in streams and trees.

As so often, Christ and Caesar – Catholicism and colonial rule – went hand in glove: these kingdoms were at least nominally Christianized and were supposed to be under the rule of the Polish kings. After repeated invasions, however, they still didn't accept anybody's overlordship – nor had they wavered in their commitment to the Pagan gods.

Again, accordingly, the call went up for a crusade. It found a response in the Teutonic Knights. This military order had an impressive (if, to modern eyes, perverse) record of 'real' crusading, having been founded in Acre at the time of the Third Crusade. Like the Knights Hospitallers, these German priests had started out tending the sick, but they had come to interpret their brief of 'care' a great deal more widely. By 1198, their role as fighting clerics had been acknowledged by the Church.

Their function in the 'Prussian Crusade' was quite clear: from about 1230 onwards they made a series of sweeps through Prussia and beyond into what are now the countries of Latvia and Lithuania. The Pope

Above: Not content with persecuting paganism, the Teutonic Knights went after Russian Orthodoxy, which led to dramatic defeat at the 'Battle of the Ice', 1242. Alexander Nevsky's tactical retreat enticed them out on to the treacherous surface of Lake Peipus where they were cut to pieces by Alexander's infantry.

had granted Prussia to the order as a 'monastic state' – in theory, at least, they were the country's rulers. In practice, this was untamed territory and they struggled to make their way against determined guerrilla opposition. Allowing themselves to be surrounded by the Samogitians at the Battle of Durbe in northwestern Lithuania in 1260, they suffered a damaging defeat that triggered an uprising across the whole of Prussia. They

Opposite: In 1377, John Wycliffe was summoned to appear before William Courtenay, Bishop of London, in Old St Paul's, to defend his 'heretical' views. Uncomfortable as he clearly was with a great deal of what Wycliffe said, Courtenay made no move to stop the wayward priest from preaching.

fought back, however, slowly and painfully restoring some semblance of order and at least the appearance of Christian observance in the region. At one raid in Scalovia, Lithuania, in 1275, the chronicler Nicholas von Jeroschin reported, the Teutonic Knights 'killed so many of the unbaptized that many drowned in their own blood'.

Reformers or Heretics?

The wealth and corruption of the medieval Church was evident to anyone with eyes to see: inevitably, impatience was going to grow. In 1177, Peter Waldo, a prosperous merchant from Lyon, France, underwent a spiritual crisis, giving away all his possessions and going on the road as a mendicant preacher. St Francis of Assisi was to do much the same thing a few years later, but he and his Franciscans went out of their way to be tactful to their superiors in the Church, managing to remain loyal – even obedient – Catholic clerics to the last. The 'Waldensians' scorned such compromise. They were openly confrontational, attacking Church leaders as representatives of the rich and powerful. Ultimately, they rejected the authority of its priests.

John Wycliffe (1320–84) was an English priest and scholar, but his words struck a chord with many of his country's less educated people, who came to hear him preach at his parish church in Lutterworth, Leicestershire. Like Waldo, Wycliffe argued that the Church had no business being rich or involving itself with the concerns of temporal government. Even in religious affairs, he argued, it had made too much of its own importance. The whole elaborate hierarchy should be scaled down, he said, and translations should be made of the Bible so that ordinary people could come to their own understanding of the Word of God and what it meant. It's easy to see why the Church might regard Wycliffe as a heretic. He denied the doctrine of 'transubstantiation': the bread and wine were not substantively changed, he said, they remained bread and wine, even as they took on the nature of Christ's body and blood. But his followers, known as 'Lollards', were seen as a threat more to secular than religious authority. The Church itself seemed extraordinarily unperturbed.

News travelled slowly in the fourteenth century, and the workings of the Church ever ground slowly. By the time the authorities in Rome had fully digested what Wycliffe was saying, he had been dead for over 20 years (seized by a stroke as he said mass in his church in Lutterworth). Not to be cheated of their punishment, they pronounced him a heretic, had his body dug up and burned and the ashes thrown into a nearby river: better late than never, they must have thought.

Left: Peter Waldo sits in pensive pose – though the Church's chief concern was that this French heretic might prove more a doer than a thinker. The 'Waldensian' line was frankly revolutionary, calling on followers to disregard the orders of a hierarchy who served 'two masters', God and Mammon (money).

HUSSITE HOSTILITIES

TODAY, THE TEACHINGS of Jan Hus are seen as paving the way for Luther and the Reformation. In his day, the Czech reformer was condemned as a heretic, even though he denied having said most of the things his clerical accusers claimed. He seems in fact to have been exercised more by the corruption he saw in the Bohemian Church.

Despite this, in 1415, he was burned at the stake. His followers, outraged, rose up against the Bohemian Crown and the Holy Roman Empire, which had the backing of Pope Martin Vl. Inevitably, he proclaimed crusades – a series of them, in 1420, 1421 and 1424. Thanks to the rebels' resourcefulness and courage, these failed to make much headway. The Hussites were helped by the hand-held cannons they used – a great leveller in the field of battle, these early firearms made infantrymen a match for the most heavily armoured knights.

A Tale of Two Trials

The Catholic Church has always shown an unholy readiness to turn a blind eye to monstrous sins committed by its political allies while upbraiding its enemies' merest faults as enormities. One example, ironically, came with the trial and execution of the 'Maid of Orléans', Joan of Arc – later, of course, to be numbered among the greatest saints. Joan, just 19 when she was executed by the English, had donned man's clothing to lead the French to a series of victories against the armies of Henry VI. Finally, though, she was defeated and captured at Compiègne.

> Asked if she knew she was in God's grace, she answered: 'If I am not, may God put me there; and if I am, may God so keep me.'

The initial intention of the English was to try her as a witch, but this proved impossible when a physical examination proved her a virgin (the conventional wisdom was that witches copulated with demons). Backed by the Bishop of Beauvais, a supporter of Henry's claims to France's throne, she was instead accused of heresy – and when this charge in its turn could not be proved, of 'insubordination and heterodoxy'. That the height of her heterodoxy appears to have been the wearing of man's clothing did nothing to assuage her guilt in the eyes of the English court.

She was burned at the stake in the town square in Rouen in 1431. Does it make it better or worse that a quarter of a century later, its fences mended with the monarchy of France, an embarrassed Catholic Church ordered a retrial of this 'heterodox' heroine? Pope Callixtus III had her case reconsidered and her original conviction was thrown out. Even so, it was not until 1920 that she was made a saint.

The War on Witchcraft

Joan of Arc was an extraordinary young woman, and virtually nothing about her case is unremarkable. One of its most unusual aspects is the attempt to brand her as a witch. This can seem surprising, given modern assumptions about 'medieval superstition'. In fact, few in the Church at this time took the idea of witchcraft seriously. The uneducated did of course swap stories of witches, warlocks, spells and curses, but clerics don't for the most part seem to have been much bothered by such notions. The idea that 'magical' powers might exist ran contrary to Catholic ideas that only God and his goodness reigned: there could be no such thing as a real 'witch' or 'wizard', so there was nothing to be feared. The great European witchhunts were to take place in the seventeenth century, a post-Reformation phenomenon, and they were invariably driven by Protestant kings and lords.

Opposite: The execution of Jan Hus in 1415 was intended to make an example of the Czech reformer. It did, but it was an example of the wrong kind. His cruel killing confirmed for his followers the outright evil of a Church he had criticized only for its worldly ways.

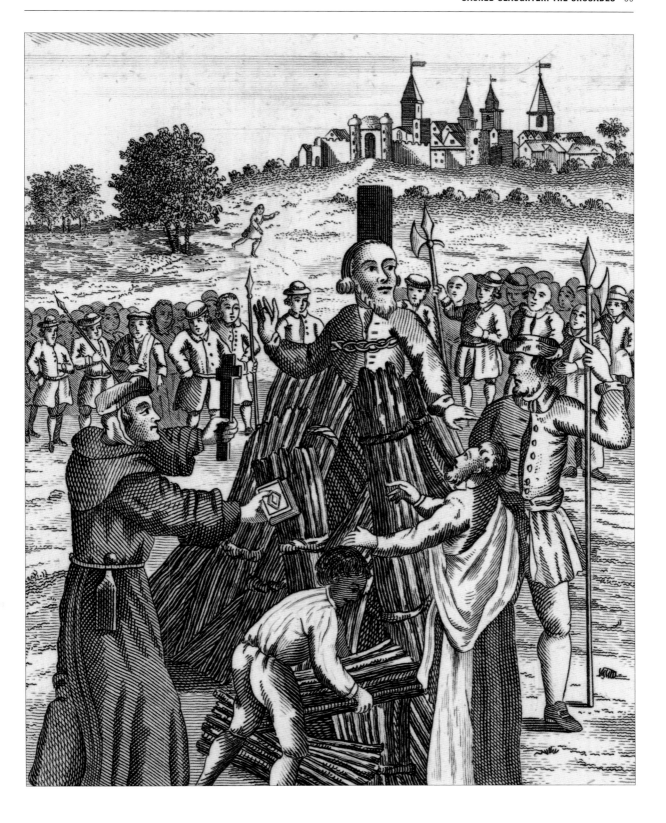

Opposite: Joan of Arc was motivated as much by her religious faith as by her French patriotism, yet the local hierarchy connived with the English over her trial. The attempt to convict her of witchcraft failing, she was sent to the stake for 'insubordination'.

Has the Catholic Church been the victim of a witchhunt, then? Not quite. Admittedly, the feeling that the modern Church has been at best sexist and arguably misogynistic in many of its attitudes has helped foster a widespread assumption that it would have been well to the fore when there were defenceless old women with cats to be persecuted. As it happens, that isn't actually how it was.

Yet the Church is not to be absolved so easily. There are clear indications that it was moving in this general direction itself in the years coming up to the Reformation. The book which was to become the manual of the Protestant witchfinders, the *Malleus Maleficarum* ('The Hammer of Wrongdoers') was written by two German Dominican priests, Henricus Institoris and Jakob Sprenger. Published with the blessing of Pope Innocent VIII in 1487, it turned centuries of Catholic orthodoxy on its head by arguing for the reality of witchcraft as a practice and insisting on the need to prosecute.

Modern feminist critics of Catholicism won't be too surprised to learn that the Dominicans saw the roots of witchcraft as lying deep in the horrifying abyss of female sexuality. 'All witchcraft stems from fleshly lust, which in women is insatiable', they wrote. Witches were confirmed in their evil beliefs and their magic powers by their couplings with the Devil. Men might have relations with him too, Henricus and Sprenger acknowledged, but women were much more highly sexed – so there were far more witches than there were wizards. Nor does it come as too much of a shock to find that witches were to be identified by breaches of feminine propriety – boldness, assertiveness, argumentativeness – even a failure to cry in the face of a prosecutor's attack.

Below: So much Catholic doctrine was unceremoniously ditched by the reformers, it's a tragic irony that they should have held on to *Malleus Maleficarum*. Though written by Dominican friars, this witchfinder's manual, the 'Hammer of Wrongdoers', was more or less ignored till taken up in post-Reformation times.

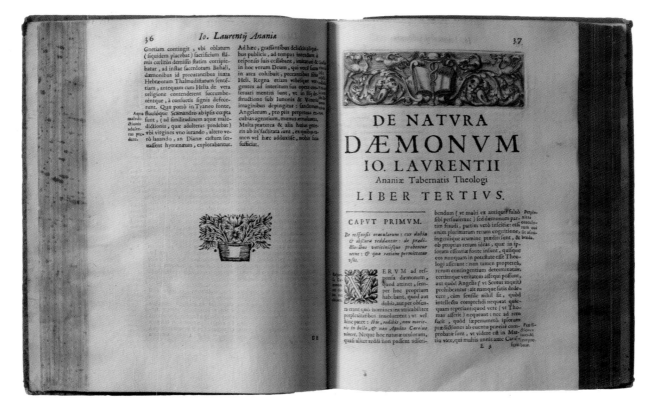

IV

SQUABBLES AND SCHISMS

The word 'Catholic' means 'universal' – and so the Church of Rome would like to be considered. But these claims have been disputed since early on. Quarrels have been frequent; wholesale splits have divided a Church that's never been more militant than in its frequent internal feuds.

'If a kingdom is divided within itself, that kingdom cannot stand.'

'One holy, Catholic and apostolic Church,' says the Creed. If only it could be so simple. Every one of those words has caused controversy at one time or another. The first word, 'one', which sounds self-evidently true, has arguably been the most hotly contested, so many have been the divisions and the splits.

Jews vs Gentiles
Scarcely, in fact, had Jesus left this Earth than his followers were bickering over the actual shape that 'Christianity' should take. The Church was to invest a great deal in the figure of St Peter – *Petrus*, the punning

'rock' on which Christ had promised to build his Church. If the head of the Apostles had had his way, however, Christ's religion might have remained a minor sect of Judaism. It had been St Paul, the 'Apostle of the Gentiles', who had argued for the Christian duty to 'go and teach all nations' and promoted Catholicism as a creed for all humankind. As a result, a great many scholars see Paul – not Peter – as Christianity's real founder after Christ himself. It was certainly he who, as proud of his Roman citizenship as he was of his Jewish identity, led the drive to centre the Church on what was then the central city of the world.

Popes and Anti-Popes
The degree to which differences of opinion and emphasis between Paul and Peter actually tipped over into outright conflict is far from clear – scholars dispute the matter to this day. One thing is for sure, though: factionalism flared up early and recurred with frequency thereafter – whether over doctrine or ritual or simply the will to power. Fighting over the papacy dates back just about to the very start of that

Opposite: St Paul preaches in an image from a sixteenth-century edition of his own 'Epistle to the Romans'. Whilst his insistence on reaching out to the Gentiles caused real controversy, it arguably made Catholicism – and Christianity in general – what it is today.

Opposite: Cyprian, Bishop of Carthage, was criticized for readmitting into his congregation those *lapsi* who'd literally 'lapsed' in the face of fierce persecution under the Emperor Decius in the early 250s. He himself stood firm, and was indeed to be martyred when the next crackdown came along in 258.

Right: A liberal *avant la lettre*, Pope Callixtus I was considered too easy-going and forgiving in his attitudes by many in the third-century Church. His critics went so far as to elect an anti-pope in opposition to his reign.

institution's history in the third century. (Despite the Gospel story, few serious historians of the Roman Catholic Church believe that St Peter was 'Pope' in anything remotely like the later sense.) The anointment of Callixtus I in 217 provoked a storm among those who saw his forgiving attitude to adulterers and remarried clergy as over-lax, and prompted the election of an 'anti-Pope' in the person of Hippolytus.

Many commentators, impatient with what they see as the hypocrisy and cynicism of the modern Church, point to the 'purity' and 'idealism' of the early Christians. Fair enough, perhaps, and yet in justice it should be noted that the supporters of these rival Popes fought deeply unedifying battles with one another in the streets of Rome. Many were killed and wounded before the quarrelling was brutally cut short by a renewed round of persecution on the part of a still-hostile Roman state. Undignified although their squabbling may have been, both presumptive pontiffs found a degree of nobility in death, each ending up as a martyr for his faith.

Not long after, in 251, the election of Pope Cornelius sparked another bitter conflict: some considered that their new leader had been craven in keeping his head down during the Emperor Trajan's Decius persecution. Novatian, elected in opposition to Cornelius' authority, was the first in a little line of anti-Popes representing this purist faction.

Doctrinal Dogfights

Later 'heresies' were often really reformist movements brought about by impatience with the bureaucracy or the corruption of what had become a big and unaccountable institution. In the early days of the Church's history, however, important points of doctrine had yet to be ironed out and there was a feeling that key ideas were up for grabs. Arianism is a good example. Its proponents argued – with Arius, an Egyptian monk – that Christ, although an inspiration, had not in fact been divine. St Ambrose led the fight against this heresy as Bishop of Milan in the fourth century, but it continued to flourish, being taken up by many within Europe's ruling class. It was finally halted

POPE JOAN

In 853, on the death of Leo IV, a female impostor is said to have ascended St Peter's throne. At first undetected in her male garb, she was finally discovered two years later, her gender revealed in the most public way possible. Suddenly, writes Jean de Mailly, during a papal procession through the streets of Rome, she gave birth to a baby before the eyes of an astonished crowd. Astounded and indignant, seeing *Il Papa* so spectacularly exposed as a mama, the post-partum pontiff was dragged off behind a horse and stoned to death. Legend had it that from that time for several centuries successive Popes were enthroned for coronation in a chair with a hole in the seat through which a groping attendant could ascertain the existence of testicles beneath their robes. The story of 'Pope Joan' was to grow in the telling, becoming a staple of anti-clerical satire in the Reformation period – and it's an intriguing little parenthesis in papal history, true or not.

Right: It's easy to see the appeal of the Pope Joan story, however questionable the evidence. Could this most patriarchal of institutions have been a matriarchy – however briefly? Protestants may have sneered, but many Catholics have wondered wistfully whether women might have a place in the hierarchy of the Church.

in its tracks in 381 by the Emperor Theodosius I's condemnation at the Constantinople Conference. That same year's Nicene Creed clearly rejected Arianism's claims. But its influence persisted in outlying regions of the West.

The fifth century brought the Nestorian Schism. An Archbishop of Constantinople, Nestorius claimed that Christ as God and Christ as Man were not two different aspects of the same being but actually two distinct persons. This heresy was taken up especially in the east, leading to the breaking-away of the so-called Assyrian Church. Monophysitism, by contrast, held that Christ had only one aspect, the divine. Its supporters were fiercely at odds with the Nestorians in the East. And on the streets of Rome itself, where what may sound like the most exquisitely rarefied

of theological discussions, were all too often pursued with sticks and knives leaving hundreds killed and wounded.

The East-West Schism

Like the Roman Empire with which by now it had become so closely identified, the Church divided naturally to some extent between East and West. And just as the 'Roman' Empire had come to be led economically and politically by its eastern outpost at Constantinople, the Western Church had played 'poor

Opposite: St Ambrose, then the Bishop of Milan, bars his cathedral door to Theodosius I in protest against a massacre he has ordered. So impressed was the Emperor at this display of quiet courage that he became the bishop's ally in his struggle against the Arian heresy.

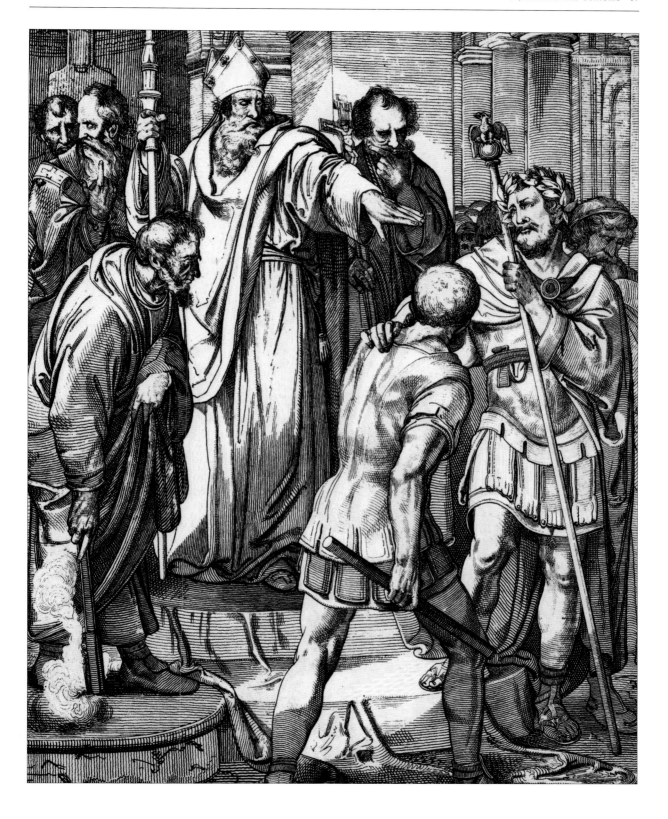

relation' to the institution in the East. All this changed with Charlemagne's coronation in 774. 'Carolus Magnus', or Charles the Great, was King of the Franks but, expanding his influence along an axis spanning the Alps from France and Germany through Italy, he created what became known as the 'Holy Roman Empire'. As the influence of this new superstate grew, so did that of the papacy in Rome, which increasingly challenged the authority of the Eastern Church.

In the centuries that followed, the fortunes of both regions fluctuated, up and down. More and more, though, they thrived or failed independently of each other. Theology followed politics and economics: by the beginning of the eleventh century, the two spheres

Below: The coronation of Carolus Magnus – 'Charlemagne' – in 774 wasn't just a magnificent occasion in itself: it tipped the whole political balance of Europe sharply westward. The Holy Roman Empire, a unique coalition between Church and imperial state, was to dominate European affairs for centuries.

> The sacred altar, fashioned from every sort of precious material and beheld as a wonder by the entire world, was broken up into bits and shared out among the soldiers – as were the other holy treasures of this splendid shrine …

were starting to go their separate ways. The differences concerned everything from the distribution of divinity among the 'Holy Trinity' and the right of the clergy to marry, to (quite seriously) the pros and cons of leavened versus unleavened bread in the Eucharist. It was indeed this last question that pushed Pope Leo IX to breaking point. In 1054, a legate from Rome laid a papal bull or decree on the altar of Constantinople's

A CRUSADE AGAINST CHRISTIANS

How DO WE do God's work without the wherewithal? Take it by force from the more vulnerable, if we are to follow the example of the Fourth Crusade. Long resented as an economic threat by rival trading centres in the West, such as Genoa and Venice, Constantinople was riven by dynastic struggles at the start of the thirteenth century. So it was that it seemed a natural next step for the leaders of the Fourth Crusade, when they found themselves short of funds to feed and pay their men, to divert to Constantinople and subject the city to a lengthy siege.

Finding a pretext in the ousting of Emperor Isaac II Angelos by his brother Alexios, they attacked the Christian capital with ferocious force. When they finally succeeded in penetrating its defences, they ran amok, embarking on an orgy of destruction. For three full days and nights they roamed the city's streets, ransacking palaces, churches and houses, looting, raping and killing as they went. Many thousands must have died: it isn't inhumanity that makes the contemporary witnesses focus on the sacrilegious damage to the city's holy places but their sense of symbolism, of a civilization and its sanctity raped and murdered.

'How', asked the Byzantine scholar Nicetas Choniates, having seen this spree of blasphemy, 'am I even to begin to describe the deeds of these wicked men? Alas, the sacred images, instead of being adored, were stamped underfoot! Alas, the holy martyrs' relics were cast down into unclean places! Then finally – one shudders even to hear such things – the consecrated body and blood of Our Lord Jesus Christ were casually pilled upon the ground or thrown about.' Even Hagia Sophia, that great central shrine of Eastern Christianity, was subjected to vandalism and humiliation of the vilest sort.

'The sacred altar, fashioned from every sort of precious material and beheld as a wonder by the entire world, was broken up into bits and shared out among the soldiers – as were the other holy treasures of this splendid shrine …

'Mules and horses were led into the innermost sanctuary of the shrine to carry away the treasure. Some, which couldn't keep their footing on the glasslike flooring, fell – and had to be stabbed and killed, so the sacred pavement ended up befouled with blood and gore.'

But the crowning insult was administered by 'a certain harlot', a companion of the victors, who 'sat in the seat of the Patriarch, singing obscenely and dancing shamelessly'. Outside in the city at large, meanwhile,

'… in the alleys, in the streets, in the churches, cries of complaint, sobbing, lamentations, grief, the groaning of men, the screams of women, wounds, rape, abductions, the forcible parting of the closest families. Nobles wandered ignominiously; the respectable elderly walked weeping, the wealthy in poverty – their riches stolen. So it was in the streets, on the corners, in the greatest church, in the lowest dives – no corner of the city was left unattacked; there was no sanctuary. Every place in every part of the city was filled with every type of crime. Oh, immortal God, how fearful men's afflictions, how terrible the distress!'

Hagia Sophia church, denouncing the actions and pronouncements of the Eastern Patriarch, Michael Kerullarios. The latter, unimpressed, immediately issued his own attack on the papacy: what has come to be known as the East-West Schism was under way.

It was to continue until 1965, at least in ecclesiastical theory, when a resolution was reached by the Patriarch and Pope Paul. To most people, though – even to believers on either side – the Catholic and Orthodox Churches had long since come to seem established as completely separate things.

A Pocket Pope

The greater the Church's wealth and spiritual authority, the more significant its political power – paradoxically, this was a source of vulnerability. Determined to annex the Church's influence to their own, Europe's kings and princes tried to push Popes

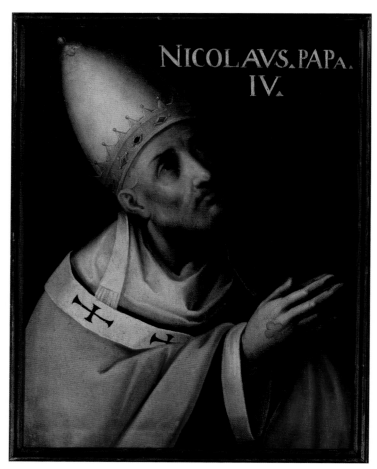

NICOLAVS.PAPA. IV.

Above: Nicholas IV might have been remembered for being the first Franciscan pope: instead he's the pontiff who let his Church be drawn into the Italian politics of his time. A genuinely unworldly man, he doesn't deserve the stigma of cynicism – a more ruthless player might have managed to steer clear.

around, intimidate and influence them. The Popes were forced into playing politics themselves.

It was a dangerous game. In 1288, Pope Nicholas IV started seeking the support of Italy's powerful Colonna family. To them, a Pope was just another pawn. In pursuance of their longstanding rivalry with the rulers of Aragón, they persuaded Nicholas to back their allies in France's House of Anjou. He accordingly crowned Prince Charles of Anjou King of Sicily and Naples. The Colonnas saw no need to surrender their special status under Nicholas' successor, Celestine V. He even moved his papal court to Naples out of deference to Charles.

Obviously, ignominiously, out of his depth, Celestine abdicated only five months into his papacy, in 1295.

Had he jumped or was he pushed? Baptized Benedetto Caetani, his successor Boniface III was a seriously intimidating figure. Celestine didn't just step down from his papal throne. He actually fled for his life and Boniface had him hunted down. He imprisoned him in a castle, where he died the following year.

Boniface was uncowed by the Colonnas, unfazed by France and unperturbed by the power of Charles II of Sicily and Naples, but his confrontational manner only ended up hastening a crisis that had arguably always been coming. Years of harassment culminated in an abduction and assassination attempt organized by Duke Sciarra Colonna and the Anjou-ally Guillaume de Nogaret in 1303 – Boniface survived what was to become known in the annals of the Church as the 'Outrage', but died of natural causes a few weeks later.

On the Move

The precedent Celestine had set by resigning from the papacy while in office wasn't to be repeated till the twenty-first century with the controversial abdication of Pope Benedict XVI (see below). But in relocating his court to Naples, it turned out he was establishing something of a trend: the 'Roman' Catholic Church became all but nomadic in the years that followed. While Boniface had restored the papal seat to Rome and his successor Benedict XI remained there, despite the pressure, the French won out after Benedict's death. As Bertrand de Got, the new Pope Clement V had been Archbishop of Bordeaux. He never so much as visited Rome and, four years into his reign in 1309, formally transferred the seat of papal power to Avignon in southern France. On behalf of France's Philip IV, he quickly moved to reinforce French domination in

Opposite: Seen here in the simple habit of a monk, Celestine V found the pomp and power of the papacy utterly bewildering. Bullied alike by Italy's noblemen and his supposed supporters in the Church, he quit his office in confusion and despair after just five months.

the wider Church by creating no fewer than 19 new cardinals from the country.

Clement V also created a splendid court – so splendid as to make many wonder what all the opulence could have to do with the Christian religion. 'Here', wrote the poet Petrarch, visiting Avignon in 1340, 'reign the successors of the poor fishermen of Galilee; they have strangely forgotten their origin. I am astounded, recalling their ancestors, to see these men weighed down by gold and dressed in purple, vaunting the spoils of princes and of nations; seeing luxurious palaces and battlemented walls, rather than a boat turned upside-down for shelter…

'Instead of sacred solitude, we get a criminal gang, with crowds of cronies; in place of sobriety, we find wild banquets…'

One such banquet, contemporary chroniclers report, had 3000 guests – although even for that number over 120 cattle, 100 calves, 900 kids, 60 pigs, 10,000 chickens, 1400 geese, 300 pike and 200 barrels of wine sounds a bit excessive.

'These are but the prelude to their orgies. I will not count the number of wives stolen or virgins deflowered.'

More specifically, fleshly sins were by no means absent. 'Prostitutes swarm on the papal beds', said Petrarch, and he went on:

'I will not speak of adultery, seduction, rape, incest: these are but the prelude to their orgies. I will not count the number of wives stolen or virgins deflowered. I will not tell of how they pressure the outraged husbands and fathers into silence, nor of the wickedness of those who willingly sell their women for gold.'

'Avignon', he summed up, was 'the foundation of anguish, the dwelling-place of wrath, the school of errors, the temple of heresy … the false guilt-laden

Left: Avignon provided the papacy with a secure base away from the politicking and intriguing of Italy. The protection – and the lavish support – of France was to come at a very high price, however: the Church faced losing all autonomy.

Σ   n.º 1.

Sergent del.   M.me De Cernel sculp.

1789

PHILIPPE IV, SURNOMMÉ LE BEL,

ROI DE FRANCE   *ET DE NAVARRE;*

né à Fontainebleau   en 1268; sacré à Reims

le 6 Janvier 1286; mort à Fontainebleau le 29 9.bre 1314.

A Paris, chez Blin, Imprimeur en Taille-Douce, Place Maubert, R.º 17, vis-à-vis la rue des 3-Portes.
A.P.D.R.

TEMPLAR TRAVESTY

OXYMORONIC AS IT may be to modern eyes, the idea of the 'military priest' seemed sensible enough in the topsy-turvy Christian thinking of the Crusading era. The 'right' of the pilgrim to visit the Holy Places of the Middle East had to be defended; with all its talk of 'turning the other cheek' and loving one's enemies, Christianity had to be upheld, if necessary, at the point of a sword. Hence the establishment of several orders of armed priests in the Holy Land (not to mention the Teutonic Knights on Christendom's northern frontier). Perhaps the most famous of these were the Knights Templar. So called on account of their founding priory on Jerusalem's Temple Mount (in fact a corner of the confiscated Al-Aqsa Mosque), the Knights Templar were tasked with providing support for pilgrims visiting Christ's City.

Given the manifold dangers of the journey – not just in the Middle East, but all the way, whether by land or sea, it made sense for one aspect of this support to involve a form of banking so that travellers didn't have to carry quantities of gold. On the back of what became a thriving business, the Templars grew extremely rich, their fortune soon attracting envious glances from Europe's monarchies. Philip IV, heavily in hock to the order, began briefing against them assiduously in the 1300s, cooking up claims of everything from financial malfeasance to sodomy.

Clement V obediently ordered a crackdown and the Knights were suppressed: 15,000 priests were arrested and many of them tortured on the rack. Highly-coloured testimony about blasphemous rituals, homosexual orgies, idol-worship and grand-scale corruption was wrung out under extreme duress. Ironically, if unsurprisingly, the main financial beneficiary was Philip IV who won twice over, writing off his debts and securing much of the Templars' wealth.

Babylon, the forge of lies, the horrible prison, the hell on Earth.'

A Faith Without Foundation

Did any of this matter? Strange as it may seem today to think of the 'Roman' Catholic Church being administered from southern France, there was arguably nothing wrong with a relocation of this kind. 'My kingdom is not of this world', Jesus had said in scripture: if the Church's realms were essentially spiritual, did it matter where its Earthly headquarters were? Initial indications were that it didn't. The Church appeared to be flourishing in France, growing steadily in splendour and in wealth – if this had brought with it some questionable moral behaviour – *pace* Petrarch, that was by no means entirely new.

Opposite: Philip IV of France was responsible for suppressing both the Knights Templar and the Jews. His motives in the two cases were much the same. Fearing both groups as brotherhoods at work within his state, he also coveted their money – both had accumulated great wealth in the banking business.

There were grounds, then, for arguing that the move to Avignon hadn't actually done the papacy too much harm – even that it had done it a degree of good. After Clement's death in 1314, six successive Popes reigned from Avignon.

This surely represented stability of a sort? Granted, it was a stability founded in immorality and decadence (Gregory XI, who reigned from 1370 to 1378, was widely believed to have been Clement VI's son). But it was still stability. The real cost – and it was to be considerable – was to the Church's autonomy. Behind the scenes, the French Crown was wielding unprecedented – and ever-growing – power.

Ultimately, indeed, it came to threaten the Church's very existence. The move to France had left the Church in Italy bereft. Rome in particular had become a city without a purpose, its role of so many centuries lost. The population had plummeted: something like 25,000 people rattled round in a vast and yet increasingly decrepit city-shell that had housed a million and a half in the early days of Christianity at the Empire's height. It was scarcely a city, more a strange and lonely

Above: Under Urban VI, the Church reasserted its independence of the French Crown – much to the vexation of Charles V. Not to be outdone, the King created his own pope and set him up in Avignon: the Church was once again divided by this 'Western Schism'.

A Proliferation of Popes

Typically, the return to Rome when it came was not to be dictated by religious reasons but by the Church's mounting fear that it might lose its lands in Italy. Instability in the country encouraged Pope Gregory XI to intervene before one of the warring aristocrats decided to help himself to the Papal States – those territories supposedly gifted to the Church under the 'Donation of Constantine' (see above). His move with key courtiers from Avignon to Rome in 1377 seems to have been more a diplomatic mission than a wholesale restoration of a Roman papacy, but in 1378 his death of a bladder problem left his retinue marooned in Rome. There, the people rose up, and it was really in response to the pressure of the mob that the cardinals held a hasty election and anointed a new – and Italian – pontiff, Pope Urban VI.

The clerics got more than they had bargained for: Urban was an exacting chief and a zealous reformer. Many in the Church's own hierarchy found themselves increasingly in sympathy with an indignant Charles V of France. The French Crown had by no means finished with a papacy it had come to look on as its own possession. Charles accordingly endowed his own 'Pope', Clement VII. Three centuries on from the great East-West Schism, the Church had been divided once again: this new 'Western Schism' carved western Christendom in two.

In the decades that followed, the split was to continue: four further 'anti-Popes' were to be elected as French counters to the Popes of Rome. Called to arbitrate in the dispute, the Council of Pisa (1408) made matters even worse – for a time the Church boasted not just two Popes but three. Finally, reason prevailed and in 1417 Pope Martin V received the recognition of the entire Catholic Church.

A Spanish Splinter-Church

Arguably the last of the Avignon Popes (although even that title isn't undisputed), Benedict XIII was well-meaning enough, as far as it went. He'd impressed his

wilderness where packs of wolves wandered along its deserted streets. Rome wasn't the only victim here. The wider Church was feeling ruined as well. Queen Bridget of Sweden had joined St Catherine of Siena in lobbying for a return to Rome. Across Christian Europe, believers were coming to feel that if the Church could be ruled from Avignon as well as it might be from Rome, it wasn't the Catholic Church to which they felt they belonged.

THE PIRATE PONTIFF

THE LAST OF the anti-Popes, John XXIII is very definitely not to be confused with the 'Blessed' Pope John XXIIII, famous as the great reformer of the modern Church. Born Baldassare Cossa on the Isle of Ischia, 'John' seems to have worked in mysterious ways to reach his clerical vocation, serving first as a pirate (two of his brothers were executed for their crimes) and then – worse, it might be argued – as a lawyer. He was in his 30s before he became a priest, and appears to have relied heavily on his old connections in Ischia's pirate bands as he bullied, schemed and possibly murdered his way up the rankings of the alternative papacy. In 1413 he was forced to flee to Florence, but was caught and compelled to appear at the Council of Constance – he again escaped and fled, but was captured, deposed and put on trial. As the English historian Edward Gibbon was to put it wryly, 'The most scandalous charges were suppressed; the Vicar of Christ was only accused of piracy, murder, rape, sodomy and incest.' Apparently, the charge sheet might have included the seduction of over 200 matrons, widows and virgins – 'to say nothing of an alarming number of nuns'.

Below: The anti-Pope John XXIII arrives at Constance after his arrest in 1413. He had briefly been one of three popes in the world. Reluctant to give up his place, he fled with his patron, Frederick IV of Austria, but was finally recaptured and forced to yield.

contemporaries by his intellect, his piety and his simple life. But, while he had commitment to his Church, he had none at all to Rome. As Pedro de Luna, he had been born in 1328 into an Aragonese nobility that had always sided with France's House of Anjou and its Avignon papacy. So he had no hesitation in accepting the succession to Clement VII as King Charles's Pope.

And all the indications are that he was a confident, capable and tolerant administrator of 'his' Church. As time went on, however, and the whole idea of the Avignon papacy became more controversial, Benedict appears to have grown defensive – and desperate to justify his reign. This, it has been suggested, was what motivated his campaign for the conversion of Spain's Jews – and his vindictive rage when his efforts abjectly failed. For centuries, believers had looked to the mass recruitment of the Jews to the cause of Christ as a sort of benignly apocalyptic turning-point in religious history. By winning what would have been an enormous coup, Benedict hoped to cast a halo around a papacy he knew had little remaining credibility in the wider Catholic Church.

Outlawing the Jewish Faith

Benedict addressed Spain's Jewish leaders in person, preaching eloquently; they heard him politely, but remained unmoved. He reacted reinstating the strictures of the Fourth Lateran Council (see above) and then going further by banning the possession and study of the Talmud altogether. Synagogues were shut

Opposite: The Western Schism wasn't to end until, at the Council of Constance in 1417, anti-Pope Benedict XIII was sent packing from his 'papacy' and excommunicated. Even then, in denial, he didn't accept what had happened, and continued with his 'reign' for several years.

Below: Not a monster – or even a mediocrity – Benedict XIII might have made a decent Pope: instead he was anti-Pope at a time when the title had lost all credibility. The less tenable his position, the more tyrannical his rule; the more wayward his measures against vulnerable targets like the Jews.

down, Jewish crafts and medical traditions were outlawed and trade between Jews and Gentiles became illegal. Attendance at Christian services three times a year was compelled. In what might be seen as a rare progressive measure, the 'official' Church rescinded all these measures in 1418.

By then the Church had rescinded his papacy too, but Benedict continued to play at being Pope, in deep denial – he even named a successor, Clement VIII. When Benedict died in 1422, he took up his title – ignored by the wider Church; he even appointed a village priest in Rodén, Zaragoza, to follow *him* – but of this putative 'Pope Benedict XIV' nothing else is known.

Lost Sheep

Church historians of this time too easily forget the wider impact of the Western Schism: if things were confused at the top, what must they have been like at national and parish level? With two or even three Popes to choose from at any given time, which was a secular ruler to acknowledge, the Roman pontiff or the French-backed Avignon Pope? Since both appointed his own bishops – and each excommunicated the others – how were priests to know if they were serving the 'true' Church? And how were ordinary men and women to be certain that the sacraments they were receiving were truly valid – were they properly married, had their babies truly been baptized and were their departed loved ones correctly laid to rest?

V
THE POWER
AND THE MONEY

As dispenser of the sacraments, the Church could claim control over the eternal destiny of its believers. Such enormous power brought enormous potential for abuse. The temptations proved too great for an institution that ultimately came to see divine salvation as something to be bought and sold.

◆

'Those who seek riches fall into … many foolish and harmful desires.'

Some would say that there's a contradiction at the very core of Catholicism: how can Christ's revolutionary message be embodied in so vast and centralized an institution as the Church? Yet how, comes the counter-question, are Christ's modern-day disciples to reach out to the world at large without considerable organization and infrastructural support? Both questions are good ones, and both have been asked repeatedly over the 2000 years of the Church's

Opposite: St Helena looks on serenely as the touch of the True Cross resurrects a woman from the dead. Constantine's mother had spent years searching for this prize. Relics such as this were to become big business in a medieval Church which was growing steadily in power and wealth.

history, without ever having been satisfactorily resolved. Catholicism's critics would object that, historically, the Church has been too ready to take the institutional route, accumulating bureaucratic complexity and amassing power and wealth – with all the corruption and complacency these things seem to bring. The Christ who drove the moneychangers from the Temple, they say, would react with fury to a 'Christianity' so firmly founded in the considerations of this world.

That's the world we have to live in, though. What's the point of a counsel of perfection in what is only too patently an imperfect reality? Who can contend with human nature (or Original Sin) without ever making the slightest stumble?

Burning Question

Despite its reputation for inflexibility, Catholicism has been too accommodating by half in some respects,

Opposite: Jacopo Tintoretto's take on Purgatory (1560), a non-scriptural innovation of the early Church with far-reaching implications for the spiritual – and material – economies. Medieval Christianity became a commerce: an endless traffic of prayers, deeds and contributions in this life in return for a remission of punishment in the next.

Above: A detail from *The Last Judgement* (1506–08), by Hieronymus Bosch, not to be confused with his earlier triptych on the same subject. Divine judgment and punishment (or reward) was a very real idea to medieval Christians, and imagined here in the most graphic terms by the artist.

it might be suggested. It's also been less dogmatic in its teachings, over time, than is generally assumed. Through much of the first millennium, for example, doctrines in key areas were pretty much a 'work in progress', continually being reassessed and overhauled. Even in what for most believers was the central area: Salvation, what it was and how it was to be achieved. Superficially, it was all straightforward enough: those who had led good lives would go on to eternal bliss; those who were lost in sin would be abandoned to the inferno in perpetuity. But what of those – and this was almost everybody, let's face it – who, while by no means diabolical in sinfulness, were at the same time less than saintly? It was clear and understandable that there could be no place in the presence of Almighty God for imperfection – but did this mean that anyone who'd fallen short in anything was going to have to burn in hell?

Opposite: Clement VI was Pope in Avignon at the time of the Black Death (1347–50), but he had arguably introduced another pestilence of his own. His papal bull *Unigenitus* (1343) had underlined the Church's right to issue (and, implicitly, to sell) indulgences.

A theological question it may have been, but it could hardly have been less empty or academic: every striving mortal faced a final judgment – and almost all did so with trepidation. The more conscientious the Christian, the harder he or she struggled to lead the virtuous life – yet the more aware they were of any falling-short. Surely, scholars started to suggest, there had to be some sort of intermediate state, for those whose lives had essentially been virtuous, even if they had faltered from time to time? By the fifth century, some were already talking of a place of temporary chastisement, in which the soul would be purged or purified by the fire, but from which it would finally be freed to dwell in heaven, for eternity.

A Place for Hope

Pope Gregory the Great had taken up the idea in the sixth century. He argued that prayerful observance or good deeds in this life could bring 'indulgence' – a remission of punishment in purgatory. It was a radical step, and it re-energized Christianity, giving good but less-than-saintly men and women new grounds for hope. Few could hope to attain perfection, but all could strive to do better in their daily lives, to throw themselves into their regimes of prayer and charitable works. The other great thing about the system was

that, since people could earn 'indulgence' not just for themselves but for their departed loved ones, it fostered a sense of solidarity between the living and the dead.

A Contractual Arrangement

What had started out as an inspirational idea was soon a fully-articulated system, with set periods of indulgence appointed for particular observances or

> Few could hope to attain perfection, but all could strive to do better in their daily lives, to throw themselves into their regimes of prayer and charitable works.

acts. So many years off for a series of masses; so many for a pilgrimage to Rome or Canterbury; so many for a donation to the poor. In very special circumstances, a 'plenary indulgence' might be granted: if the receiver died in that moment, his or her soul would pass instantaneously to heaven.

The idea of a carefully worked-out sliding scale of remissions strikes us as strangely mechanistic now, maybe, but there was nothing intrinsically wrong or wicked about it, it must be said. Quite clearly, it gave ordinary believers a real spiritual incentive to which they could respond: it was good for them, good for the Church and good for the poor and the sick they were

A MOVEABLE FEAST

THE IDEA OF the 'jubilee' harked back to Biblical times, when the 49th year (the last of seven seven-year cycles) was held to mark the cancelling of debts and the curtailment of terms of slavery. Boniface's reintroduction of the tradition appears to have been more or less entirely opportunistic.

It certainly paid off: pilgrims flocked to Rome and, according to one contemporary observer, were so generous with their donations 'that two clerics stood day and night by the altar of St Peter's, gathering

up the coins with rakes'. Although Boniface had announced that these 'new' jubilees were to be once-in-a-century events, his successors couldn't bear to wait that long: a second was held by Clement VI in 1350.

The gaps grew even shorter: another jubilee followed in 1390, after which the gap was changed to 33 years to reflect the span of Jesus' life. Finally, after further adjustment up and down, the term was set at 25 years in 1450, and so it has continued ever since.

Above: Pope Boniface VIII presides over a council of cardinals. He did much to increase the Church's wealth and power. Asserting the primacy of papal authority over that of temporal rulers, he staged an impressive show of strength in the first ever Jubilee (1300).

inspired to help. At the same time, though, the system was only too clearly open to abuse: the temptation was always there for the Church to harness it to worldly ends. When Pope Boniface VIII proclaimed a jubilee for 1300, for example, he promised a plenary indulgence to those who made the pilgrimage to Jerusalem that year. Two million people heeded his call. The benefit his jubilee did in reinvigorating the wider Church must be set against the suspicion that he was exploiting the (good) faith of his flock and staging a show of strength

for his political enemies in Rome. At the same time he could be viewed as promoting his own personality-cult: by all accounts Boniface dressed himself in the traditional garb of the Roman Caesars, insisting that he was an Emperor just as much as he was Pope.

Salvation for Sale

More problematic was the financial note, which may have been innocent enough to start with but was insidiously – and possibly completely – corrupting over time. It began with the payment of fees for masses offered up for the souls of the dead. This was another way of gaining them remission, and the token sums paid were a welcome supplement to the incomes of poor parish priests. Gradually the practice spread, however, as the Church came first to rely on the contributions it gained this way and then to start exploiting its people's piety. The poor were bullied into paying for prayers, the wealthy effectively bribed with offers of an easy afterlife. Soon high prelates and great religious houses were growing rich on the proceeds of what amounted to an indulgence industry.

And an 'industry' it was – so much so that it can be seen as a major branch of the medieval economy. The 'Church Suffering' (as the souls in purgatory were called) can be seen as having formed an economic community with the living. The endowment of monasteries, churches, almshouses, gifts of land: these were gifts bequeathed by the dying to those who followed after. Golden chalices, jewelled reliquaries, stained-glass windows, woodcarvings – all the

splendour of the medieval Church was underwritten by the dead. We have this system to thank for Cologne Cathedral, Notre Dame and all the other glories of the Gothic period – but it's some way removed from what most of us would regard as spirituality or religious faith. The Church was altogether unabashed about the relationship between the payment of money and the buying of salvation: in 1245, when England's King Henry III proposed rebuilding Westminster Abbey, he won the approval of Pope Innocent IV. More than this, he won a papal promise that anyone making a

Below: Forgiveness for sale – priests and Church officials at a medieval market sell indulgences. Whilst Protestant propagandists undoubtedly talked up the crassness of the commerce, it can't be claimed that the criticism was in its essentials wrong.

contribution to the project would receive 20 days' indulgence from the sufferings of purgatory.

By the fourteenth century, indulgences were being openly bought and sold. In 1344, Clement VI issued 200 plenary indulgences in England alone, 'earned' entirely by financial endowments to the papacy. Among the various shysters and charlatans mingling with the more pious pilgrims in Geoffrey Chaucer's *Canterbury Tales* is a professional 'Pardoner'. In his saddlebag he carried a sheaf of printed 'pardons … hot from Rome', ready for signing and distributing to anyone who will pay his price.

Macabre Mementoes

Chaucer's Pardoner is also furnished with a grotesque range of 'relics'. These were basically souvenirs of the saints, or of the life of Christ himself. They were a great deal more than keepsakes, though. The whole Canterbury Pilgrimage was a testament to the power such

Right: Geoffrey Chaucer (c.1343–1400) painted a vivid poetic picture of a medieval scene in which the Church was as much a part of economic as of religious life. His *Canterbury Tales* underlines the importance of pilgrimage as not just a spiritual but a social and commercial enterprise.

items were believed to have. Six days after St Thomas Beckett had been savagely struck down by King Henry II's men in Canterbury Cathedral in 1170, it was said a blind woman had touched his bloodstained garment and promptly had her sight restored.

Beckett's tomb immediately became a place of pilgrimage: people flocked to Canterbury throughout the Middle Ages; just as they did to the supposed burial sites of Saint James at Compostela, in Galicia, Spain, and of St Andrew in the cathedral of St Andrew's, Scotland. Pilgrimage became big business – and monasteries and churches that housed prestigious tombs raked in huge sums in offerings and mass-fees.

You didn't have to have a whole tomb to have a sacred shrine, however: a 'holy relic' could be as small as a scrap of cloth or a fingernail. Many were held by religious houses, which could become important places of pilgrimage in their own right as a result. Others might be bought by individuals. It was, of course, impossible to have any real certainty as to provenance. Swindlers flourished in these most credulous of times. So, for example, 'in his bag', Chaucer's Pardoner:

A SETTLING OF ACCOUNTS

CONSIDERING THE LIFE of John Baret, a fifteenth-century merchant from Bury St Edmunds, and going through the (astonishingly detailed) provisions of his will, historian Carl Watkins in his book, *The Undiscovered Country: Journeys Among the Dead*, shows how systematic – even businesslike – he was in approaching his eternity. In exactly the same spirit as

that in which he settled Earthly debts, he approached the obligations he assumed he had to God and to his own immortal soul, allocating money for monuments, and buying masses in advance to ensure the salvation in the life to come. In just this spirit, others gave gifts of land, contributed carvings, stained-glass windows or helped towards the construction of new chapels.

... had a pillow-case,
He claimed was Our Lady's veil;
He said he had a strip of the very sail
Saint Peter had, when he went
Upon the sea – before Christ called him.
He had a latten cross all set with stones,
And in a glass reliquary he had some pig's bones.
But, with these 'relics', when he found
Some poor peasant living on the land,
He could make more money in a single day
Than that poor wretch might make in two
whole months...

Passing off the pig's bones as belonging to some important saint – or even, perhaps, to Christ himself – he would have been able to charge an uncritical customer a small fortune for the privilege of touching or kissing this sacred 'relic'.

Chaucer's Pardoner is of course a satirical creation, but it would be wrong to assume that he was outlandishly exaggerated. Hairs of John the Baptist; foreskins of the infant Christ; vials of the Virgin's milk; her girdle; Mary Magdalen's comb; some of St Peter's beard; an arm of the Apostle James – all these things and countless more were in circulation in medieval Europe's relics-market, in good faith. And it wasn't just the poor and uneducated who kept the commerce going. Especially when especially important relics (fragments of the 'True Cross', for example) could

Below: We shouldn't underestimate the hold of faith over the medieval mind. The arrogant Emperor Henry IV bullied Pope Gregory VII shamelessly – but crumpled under threat of excommunication. After a penitential walk in the winter cold to the papal castle at Canossa, he fasted outside for three days, begging for forgiveness.

THE INVESTITURE CONTEST

IN SETTING A financial value on religious offices, corruption couldn't help but jeopardize the independence of the Church, for, unsurprisingly, secular rulers wanted their share of the spoils. With money and power alike at stake, the tussle between Popes and Kings was bound to be a long and bitter one, although it reached its height in the 'Investiture Contest' of the eleventh and twelfth centuries. The controversy was over who got to 'invest' or appoint a country's bishops and senior clergy, with all that meant in access to income and influence. Kings and princes argued, not unreasonably, that these officials were being appointed to serve the people of their kingdoms; Popes pointed out – again not unreasonably – that they were to be officers of the Church. In 1076, the Holy Roman Emperor, Henry IV, having goaded Pope Gregory VII too far, was excommunicated – expelled from the Church. He had to make the penitential 'Walk to Canossa' to beg the Pope's forgiveness.

The Concordat of Worms (1122) gave monarchs the right to invest the bishops they chose within their kingdoms, on condition that they acknowledged the supreme spiritual authority of the papacy. But a real and enduring peace between Popes and Emperors was to prove elusive.

command such astronomical prices. King Louis IX of France (St Louis) spent 40,000 livres building his spectacular gothic Saint Chapelle on the Île de la Cité

> Once the precedent was established that a religious office was a prize, all pretense of it being a position to be earned was quickly lost.

in Paris – but he'd paid more than three times that amount for the holy relics (including the Crown of Thorns from the Crucifixion) the chapel had been designed to house.

Ecclesiastical Enterprise

An important church or monastery was a major moneymaking concern: cash donations, large and small, were just the start. Lands bequeathed by the dying might be rented out – or farmed by monks on behalf of the community; and there was income from local taxes and peasants' tithes. Senior positions in the Church were eminently covetable for this reason, and there was brisk competition for the most lucrative 'livings' – for, then as now, some parishes, dioceses or monasteries were much more profitable than others.

The result was a flourishing trade in church offices – this was considered a sin in its own right, that of 'simony', with its own special circle of damnation in Dante's Hell. (It took its name from Simon Magus, or 'Simon the Magician', the Samaritan sorcerer who, in the Acts of the Apostles 8: 9–24, tried to buy the ability to summon up the Holy Ghost – which he imagined to be some sort of magic 'spell' – from Saints John and Peter.) Despite regular denunciations, simony had a way of being self-perpetuating and of spreading itself through the whole Church structure, since, having paid out for their own positions, senior prelates felt the need to take bribes from those seeking situations further down the ladder.

One kind of corruption let in another. Once the precedent was established that a religious office was a gift or prize, all pretense of it being a position to be earned, and then upheld with responsibility, was quickly lost. It was no coincidence that Pope Nicholas III, denounced by Dante as the chief of the simonists, was also guilty of nepotism on an all but heroic scale, making three of his closest relations into cardinals.

Opposite: The sin of simony – selling Church offices – inverted true religious values, prioritizing material over spiritual gain. Hence the punishment envisaged for the simoniacs in Dante's great poem, the *Divine Comedy*, in which offenders have to spend eternity upside-down in holes, writhing and flailing in endless fire.

VI

ENFORCING ORTHODOXY: THE INQUISITION

Can any real religious faith be imposed by force and through fear of torture and execution? Faced with a threefold threat from crypto-Islam, secret Judaism and – most of all – new Christian 'heresies', the Catholic Church determined to do its best to try.

◆

'Judge not, that you be not judged.'
— *MATTHEW 7: 1*

One day in 1620, a certain William Lithgow, a Scottish travel writer in search of colourful material, got more than he bargained for when he was arrested as a spy in Málaga. As a foreigner – and a Protestant – he was automatically suspicious in a Spain that for several centuries now had been in the grip of the 'Holy Office' – better known now as the 'Inquisition'. Lithgow's story is unusual only in having happened to an English-speaking writer with the contacts to get the facts out to the outside world.

Opposite: St Dominic de Guzman (1170–1221) overseas at *auto-da-fé*, in this painting by Spanish artist Pedro Berruguete (1450–1504). The scene takes place in thirteenth century, though the characters dress in the manner of the late fifteenth century.

It's worth setting out here at some length, as a sort of case study in the cruelty of which the Inquisition was capable – just as a matter of routine:

'About midnight, the sergeant and two Turkish slaves released Mr. Lithgow from his then confinement, but it was to introduce him to one much more horrible. They conducted him through several passages, to a chamber in a remote part of the palace, towards the garden, where they loaded him with irons, and extended his legs by means of an iron bar above a yard long, the weight of which was so great that he could neither stand nor sit, but was obliged to lie continually on his back. They left him in this condition for some time.'

The 'Turks' in this story were almost certainly North African Moors, prisoners-of-war enslaved by Spain. It is ironic that the only kindness Lithgow was to receive in his time in the Spanish gaol would be from African prisoners of this kind.

'The next day he received a visit from the governor, who promised him his liberty, with many other advantages, if he would confess being a spy; but on his protesting that he was entirely innocent, the governor left him in a rage, saying, "He should see him no more until further torments constrained him to confess"; commanding the keeper, to whose care he was committed, that he should permit no person whatever to have access to, or commune with him; that his sustenance should not exceed three ounces of musty bread, and a pint of water every second day; that he shall be allowed neither bed, pillow, nor coverlid. "Close up (said he) this window in his room with lime and stone, stop up the holes of the door with double mats: let him have nothing that bears any likeness to comfort." … In this wretched and melancholy state did poor Lithgow continue without seeing any person for several days…'

> … he lay on the rack for above
> five hours, during which time
> he received above sixty different
> tortures of the most hellish
> nature …

Taken to another place for further interrogation, Lithgow was freed from his shackles ('which put him to very great pains, the bolts being so closely riveted that the sledge hammer tore away half an inch of his heel') only to be 'stripped naked, and fixed upon the rack'.

'It is impossible to describe all the various tortures inflicted upon him. Suffice it to say that he lay on the rack for above five hours, during which time he received above sixty different tortures of the most hellish nature; and had they continued them a few minutes longer, he must have inevitably perished.

'These cruel persecutors being satisfied for the present, the prisoner was taken from the rack, and his irons being again put on, he was conducted to his former dungeon, having received no other nourishment than a little warm wine, which was given him rather to prevent his dying, and reserve him for future punishments, than from any principle of charity or compassion.

'As a confirmation of this, orders were given for a coach to pass every morning before day by the prison, that the noise made by it might give fresh terrors and alarms to the unhappy prisoner, and deprive him of all possibility of obtaining the least repose.

'In this loathsome prison was poor Mr. Lithgow kept until he was almost devoured by vermin. They crawled about his beard, lips, eyebrows, etc., so that he could scarce open his eyes; and his mortification was increased by not having the use of his hands or legs to defend himself, from his being so miserably maimed by the tortures. So cruel was the governor, that he even ordered the vermin to be swept on him twice in every eight days.'

The idea of the Inquisition casts almost as disturbing a shadow now, in the mythic imagination, as it did in its fearful heyday – albeit then as a grim reality. There is something uniquely terrifying about an organization that sets out so coldly and deliberately to torture, maim and kill in the cause of 'God'.

From Black Legend to Whitewash

The first Inquisition had been set up in southern France in the thirteenth century, in hopes of stemming the rising tide of Catharism in the years before the Albigensian Crusade. An anti-Waldensian Inquisition followed in Italy, but thereafter the 'Holy Office' waned in importance, to be revived in Spain and Portugal (and their overseas colonies) from the late fifteenth century. More of these ecclesiastical courts for suppressing heresy were constituted in France and Italy during the Reformation.

Modern historians have been quick to point to the *Leyenda Negra*, or 'Black Legend' – the stream of anti-Spanish and anti-Papist propaganda put out by the Protestant nations of northern Europe in early modern times. They're right. In the sixteenth and seventeenth centuries, sectarian suspicions ran as deep as ideological mistrust was to in the Cold War decades of the twentieth century. And there's no real doubt that this was indeed the case – that highly-coloured conspiracy theories were rampant, along with lurid accounts of colonial atrocities, and prisoners subjected

Opposite: Lanark-born William Lithgow, the 'Wonderful Traveller', had indeed roamed extraordinary distances in his time. He had walked the length and breadth of Europe – making further forays into the Middle East and North Africa – before he famously fell foul of the Inquisition in southern Spain.

to terrible tortures. Yet there's no real doubt either that the Cold War decades saw CIA 'dirty tricks' and NATO spy-rings – not to mention Soviet human-rights abuses on a colossal scale. This or that example may have been exaggerated – even dreamed up from nowhere by a Protestant pamphleteer in Britain or the Netherlands – but the Inquisition existed every bit as surely as the GULAG did.

The 'Rules of Torture'

But the image we have of it is a caricature, revisionist historians have objected – and of course they have been right, up to a point. Modern researchers point to the painstaking documentation kept by the Holy Office; the elaborate procedures that had to be followed before violent methods might be applied. Strict rules

governed the Inquisition and its workings: those accused of heresy were to be given several weeks' warning and a chance to recant before being subjected to any sort of questioning – still less any sort of torture. The danger of malicious denunciation was recognized and safeguards in place to prevent mischievous prosecutions. The inquisitors themselves were priests in orders, sworn on their honour to carry out their work in the cause of God and not for any personal pleasure or advantage.

Scholars have also underlined the fact that, although administered by the Church, the Inquisition worked with the temporal authorities. In many cases, indeed, it seems to have been the state that took the lead. Monarchs always had an interest in enforcing conformity and were happy enough to claim divine

Opposite: Stretched to sinew-shredding, joint-cracking agony on an ever-tightening cranking wheel, a man suspected of harbouring heretical views is quizzed by the Inquisition. Almost literally 'grilled', he has flames applied to his feet to encourage cooperation.

Below: Heretics are led out to face the flames having been convicted at an *auto-da-fé* or 'act of faith'. Such ceremonies were conducted across the Spanish-speaking world in the sixteenth and seventeenth centuries. This one was conducted at Córdoba, in southern Spain.

Above: St Francis of Assisi receives the blessing of Innocent IV for his 'rule' – the code for his new order of mendicant friars. But the very same pope had sanctioned another rule – that allowing the Inquisition to extract the 'truth' by torture; thousands were to suffer unspeakable agonies in consequence.

Gospels – even the notorious admonition to 'Render to Caesar what is due to Caesar' – could have justified the application of rack and pinions to prisoners, however 'heretical' their views. Torture wasn't an abuse of inquisitorial procedure, it was its very basis – it had been ever since its explicit approval by Pope Innocent IV in 1252.

'Banality of Evil'

As for the bureaucratic scrupulousness of the Holy Office, this aspect of the Inquisition is only underlined by the meticulously itemized invoices sent to many grieving families, which demanded payment for interrogation, imprisonment, transportation and execution costs.

The reality, in any case, seems to be that such as they were these procedures were widely disregarded. Equipped with all the powers of judges, juries and executioners, and more or less completely free of any outside supervision or any need for transparency, the Inquisitors did what men in such a privileged position have invariably done throughout history – took the utmost advantage of the cruel powers they had.

Take Inquisitor Diego Rodríguez Lucero of Córdoba who, in 1506, was accused of having denounced and executed one of the city's leading citizens to gain access to his wife. She was forced to remain with him as his mistress – along, it was said, with another girl, whose parents had been branded 'heretics' for resisting his designs.

Some 20 years later, Granada's city councillors wrote an official letter to King Charles V objecting that inquisitors were using their powers over husbands and fathers to force wives and daughters into sexual submission on a systematic basis. This sort of collective response was rare enough: few were rash enough to make individual complaints. One man who did, in

sanction for doing so. After the Reformation, moreover, religion took on a political aspect. A Protestant was no longer just a heretic but a dangerous subversive – potentially, the agent of a foreign state.

This hardly counts as an excuse, of course. That the Church had allowed itself to get so close to the Earthly authorities of the time, identifying their interests so completely with its own, is something of an indictment in itself. It's certainly hard to see what in Christ's

SHOW, TELL AND TORTURE

THERE'S GOOD REASON for the Inquisition's mythic role as the archetypal example for all subsequent programmes of repression: it went about its work in a cold, calculating and organized way. It also understood, as others didn't quite yet, the value of psychological terror and trauma: arguably, the torture began with the first serving on the suspect of a summons to appear. The weeks of delay and the fear they instilled were enough to break the nerve of waverers – many recanted 'heretical' beliefs before they'd even been brought before the court. (On the basis of what might seem relatively trivial admissions, new areas of enquiry might easily be opened up, and the names of new suspects brought before inquisitors.) Others cracked at the point when – as was routinely done at a preliminary session – they were given a 'tour' of the torture chamber and shown the instruments that might be used.

The most important of these – the central mechanism of the inquisitorial process, it might be said – was the *potro* (literally 'colt' or 'horse'):

the rack. Basically a long trestle table on which the prisoner was laid out flat, his ankles shackled, it had a ratcheting mechanism at the other end so the victim could be stretched out by his (or her) arms – to a bone-breaking point and well beyond. It was typically supplemented by the application of a cloth gag on to which water was poured to simulate drowning (the modern 'waterboard'). Alternatively (or additionally) a standing prisoner might have his arms chained behind his back and then be hoisted up into the air. This excruciating position (the 'hanging aeroplane', to modern torturers) left the dangling body fully exposed to attack by beating or by flogging, or to a cruel succession of bone-jarring, muscle-tearing drops.

Below: Torture wasn't just a punishment for the Holy Office, it was an integral part of the process, as Alessandro Magnasco's painting *A Court of the Inquisition* (c.1710) makes clear. The whole system was hideously paradoxical in its workings, an incongruous combination of bureaucracy and brutality.

Murcia in 1560, seeing an inquisitor openly consorting with the widow of a man he'd sent to the stake, was himself promptly denounced as a Jew and executed.

A Ferocious 'Faith'

If the Inquisition's abuses had ended at torture they would have been bad enough, but the Holy Office claimed the right of life and death. And not just of death but of divine judgement: the public show-trial and execution it staged for the confirmed heretic, the *auto-da-fé* (or 'Act of Faith') was a ritualized enactment of the Last Judgment. The actual fire in which the unfortunate prisoner was burned at the stake only too obviously symbolized the flames of hell – the inquisitors were quite literally pre-judging the eternal destiny of those they killed. Or, rather, those the executioners killed, because as clerics they were ever-mindful of God's commandments – far be it from any churchman to take a life.

> Most prisoners weren't actually killed by fire but by garrotting at the stake – their consumption by the flames was more symbolic.

At the last moment, then, the prisoner was released (the Spanish word, literally, meant 'relaxed') to lay-executioners who actually carried out the dirty work. Most prisoners weren't actually killed by fire but by garrotting at the stake – their consumption by the flames was more symbolic. In some cases, though, where heretics had held out against their torturers with obstinacy (or courage), they might indeed have to endure the first flames alive.

Large crowds came to see what where by any standards grand and carefully choreographed spectacles (300,000 attended one in Valladolid in 1559). They were drawn no doubt by vulgar curiosity and the desire for a sadistic frisson, but also by the implicit underlining the event gave of the reassuringly rigid

Left: The *auto-da-fé* became an essential aspect of Iberian (and Latin American) culture. Held in public squares, it played a part in cementing civic and social life. Vast crowds came out to see what was at once a lurid spectacle and a solemn, sacred ceremony.

WORTHY OF THE NAME

THE SPANISH INQUISITION had first been established in Aragón in the thirteenth century, but it came into its own in the fifteenth under Ferdinand and Isabella, the 'Catholic Monarchs'. They bore that title because by their marriage they had brought the realms of Navarra, Aragón and Castile together into a single 'Spain'. (The word 'Catholic' originally meant 'universal', 'all-embracing' – hence indeed its use for the Church of Rome.) But Ferdinand and Isabella were also 'Catholic' in the now more obvious sense of supporting the Catholic Church in all its beliefs and values – including its ugliest ones. They welcomed the Holy Office to their kingdom, granting it far-reaching powers and privileges, using ecclesiastical structures as the basis for what we would now consider a 'police state'.

Below: Torquemada, the Inquisition's torturer-in-chief, had a special rapport with Spain's 'Catholic Monarchs', Ferdinand and Isabella. Tireless in his hunting-down of heresy in all its forms, he was particularly paranoid about the country's Jews. It was at his urging that they were driven out of Spain.

orderliness of the moral universe. The 'achievement' of the Inquisition was the sense of security it created for the credulous and the conformist in a time when all the certainties of life and belief were being questioned.

It's not for nothing that the 'Spanish Inquisition' has come to have more of a mythic aura than its equivalents in Italy and France. Only in Spain did the Holy Office make common cause quite so completely with a state so resolutely bent on a near-totalitarian programme of centralization and social and cultural policing.

Unmingling the Melting Pot

The Islamic kingdom of al-Andalus had been a beacon of civilization, style and culture in a Western Europe that had still been very backward in many ways. Science, scholarship, literature and art had flourished in an atmosphere of enlightenment and tolerance in which all sections of the community had felt free to live and worship in their own very different ways. In recent years, radical historians have suggested that al-Andalus was some sort of utopia, a paradigm for what the

Above: Ferdinand and Isabella receive the surrender of Granada's Muhammad II or Boabdil (from 'Abu Abdullah') after the fall of Spain's last sultanate in 1492. Coinciding with the expulsion of the Jews – and, of course, Columbus' discoveries – the event opened a new chapter in the history of Spain.

modern multicultural society might be. This is perhaps an over-optimistic view: Christians and Jews in Muslim Spain might have begged to differ, disdained as they were by Islamic authorities who were quick to subject them to petty harassment, and saw them as a 'soft' population always ready to be milked for taxes.

Yet it's true that, basically, by the standards of this and later times, al-Andalus did enjoy comparatively easy-going community relations. The authorities certainly never mounted anything remotely resembling a general persecution of Jews or Christians, nor did they try to prevent their living and worshipping as they liked. Intermarriage, while not encouraged, wasn't stopped; commercial and cultural relations spanned the divides; 'live and let live' was the order of the day.

Opposite: Like her friend St John of the Cross, the mystic Teresa of Ávila (pictured) was partly of Jewish descent. Sixteenth- and seventeenth-century Spanish spirituality was a psychodrama, its intensity deriving both from the country's hybrid heritage and from official attempts to suppress its legacy.

So when, in the fifteenth century, Ferdinand and Isabella came along and tried to carve out a Catholic monoculture in Spain, they found themselves facing a very challenging task indeed. While Muslim Spain officially came to an end with the Siege of Granada in 1492 – the same year in which the last of the country's openly-observant Jews were expelled – the new Spain still found itself with major Muslim and Jewish 'problems'. Only by force and by the fear of pain and death could members of these groups be compelled to convert. And even when they did, their good faith was always to be suspect – with good reason, because, naturally enough, many did make a show of obedience to save their own lives and their families' without actually experiencing any real shift in religious loyalties.

Crypto-Jews and -Muslims undoubtedly did exist, going through the motions of Catholic observance while secretly continuing with their old ancestral ways. At the same time, though, there were a great many genuinely pious Christians of Jewish or Islamic heritage who never could find full acceptance. A rumour about a grandparent or great-uncle might easily be enough to guarantee a life dogged by suspicion from busybody neighbours or officious local priests. Such was the paranoia abroad in Spain that even the holiest of Christians came under suspicion – including such celebrated figures as Saint Teresa of Avila and Saint John of the Cross. Both had been born into *converso* ('convert') families, although both had been brought up in – and had taken passionately to – the creed of Christ. But the more apparently blameless people were, paradoxically, the more suspicion they risked arousing in a paranoid nation in which the quest for religious and cultural purity became obsessive.

Racial Hygiene

Limpieza – 'cleanness' – it was called, and it was regarded as residing in the blood, a more unusual association than might be imagined in the fifteenth century. The sort of pseudo-scientific 'race theory' that was to foreshadow the emergence of Nazism in the modern age was more or less entirely alien to earlier times. In Spain, however, the Inquisition introduced a code of *limpieza de sangre* – pure-bloodedness – that looked forward to the Nuremberg Laws of 1935. At a stroke, the legislation created a sort of second-class citizenship: the 'New Christians', it was reasoned, weren't quite Christian after all. Anybody seeking public office, a place in the priesthood or even a matrimonial alliance with an 'Old Christian' family could expect to have to swear an oath of *limpieza* – and

Below: Spanish anxieties about contaminating strands of Jewish and Muslim ancestry transferred 'naturally' to a New World in which relations with native populations (and African slaves) were inevitable. The result was a blood-based hierarchy in which 'pure'-white *criollos* (creoles) clearly outranked 'mixed' *mestizos* like those seen here.

THE GRAND INQUISITOR

SPAIN'S MOST IMPORTANT inquisitor, and to this day a byword for all that's fanatical and cruel in intellectual and political repression, Tomás de Torquemada was born in Valladolid in 1420. From boyhood he saw his vocation as a religious one – although he quickly came to see that religious orthodoxy had political aspects too. He met the future Queen Isabella when he was in his forties and she was just a teenage princess, but became her mentor pretty much from that time on. (It even seems to have been his idea that she should marry Prince Ferdinand of Aragón, creating a powerful – and super-Catholic – kingdom in the heart of Spain.)

The Grand Inquisitor from 1483, he literally 'wrote the book' on inquisitorial practice – the *Compilation of Instructions for the Office of the Holy Inquisition* – although it wasn't actually to be published till the end of the sixteenth century. No matter, its strictures governed procedures on everything from sorcery to sodomy – whatever the charge, torture was to be at the heart of Inquisitorial practice. Although known as the 'Hammer of Heretics', Torquemada showed particular zeal and ruthlessness in rooting out crypto-Muslims and *Marranos*. Was this fanaticism founded in self-hatred? Some scholars have certainly suspected as much, pointing to the presence of known Jews among the Inquisitor's ancestral connections.

Left: Torquemada's tome, the *Compilation of Instructions for the Office of the Holy Inquisition* didn't just provide tips for torturers. By codifying practices, setting down procedures for interrogation in elaborate detail, it lent an air of legitimacy to what was at bottom a brutal system.

Opposite right: *Damned by the Inquisition*, by nineteenth-century painter Eugenio Lucas Velázquez. The Inquisition cast a long shadow over the collective consciousness of Catholic Spain, providing material for painters for many centuries after its end.

to have his or her antecedents carefully researched.

It wasn't racism, technically – or even actually, indeed, given that the very idea of 'race' hadn't yet been formulated. A Jewish or Muslim ancestry was suspect because it suggested the risk of a secret loyalty to an alien religion, not because it made an individual different in some more essential way. At the same time, though, the location of this *limpieza* in the blood did obviously imply some intrinsic, physiological difference between 'Old' and 'New' Christians of the sort that in later centuries would have been rationalized as 'race'. The ease with which the doctrine was afterwards able to be transferred to the American colonies to distinguish between *criollos* or 'creoles' of pure Spanish blood and those *mestizos* (mixed-race Spanish and Indian) or *mulatos* (Spanish and African) suggests that it was already a sort of racism-in-waiting.

Coming Out in the Wash

In Spain itself, though, the emphasis was always upon religious backsliding. Even if a *converso* was faithful now, that didn't mean he or she could be relied on to remain so. Hence, the conscientious Spanish servant would always be on the lookout for some sign that her employer was avoiding pork chorizo; or a master might note if a servant was mumbling during household prayers. Just as those who *were* pursuing a forbidden faith in secret learned to hide their ritual practices with the utmost subtlety, conventional Catholics grew hugely sophisticated in detecting (real or imaginary) lapses.

Like that of María de Mendoza, a young *morisca* woman from Cuenca in central Spain. She was seen by a witness to draw a jar of water from a well then take it home where, kneeling naked, she washed her hair and body down. Given that Islamic observance does

> Just as those who pursued a forbidden faith in secret learned to hide their practices, conventional Catholics grew hugely sophisticated in detecting lapses.

prescribe ritual ablutions prior to praying or reading in the Quran, it's perhaps not surprising that washing should have been viewed askance, suggests historian Toby Green. In an age when mass-produced soap still lay several centuries in the future, and standards of personal hygiene were necessarily rough and ready, washing was not something most people generally did.

A New World of Persecution

Its work in attacking Catharism done – or, rather, superseded by a policy of virtual genocide – the French Inquisition dropped from sight. It was never to rival the

Below: Heretics convicted by the Inquisition process to their place of public execution in Lisbon in this engraving. The crimes of the Portuguese Inquisition have been overshadowed by those of Spain's, but they were every bit as grave – and as integral to the state.

Right: Christopher Columbus arrives in America – a heroic scene, but one overflowing with historical ironies. The 'benefits' of the European civilization he brought with him were to include conquest and enslavement, deadly epidemics and, of course, the plague of Christian piety, cruelly enforced.

scale of the Spanish or Portuguese Inquisitions in the early-modern period. Or their reach, because of course this was a time in which Spain and Portugal were opening up new territories in the Americas. They took the Inquisition with them wherever they went. More important than the desire to strike fear into (already well and truly terrorized) native populations in the New World was the fear that, far from home, Europeans would stray from the straight and narrow. How was the Church to stop the spread of Protestantism among an independent-minded community of settlers across the ocean? What was to stop 'New Christians' from reverting to Muslim or *Marrano* type? Mexico City, the capital of 'New Spain', became its capital of cruelty, with regular round-ups of 'heretics' and spectacular public *autos-da-fé*. The same was true, although to a lesser extent, in the Portuguese colonies of Brazil.

The Roman Inquisition

Italy, the Church's home country, was no more immune than anywhere else to the plague of heresy, and here too the Holy Office did its work. But it never managed to make common cause with the secular

MORISCOS AND MARRANOS

EVERYONE IN SIXTEENTH-CENTURY Spain paid at least lip service to Catholic orthodoxy. It was more than one's life was worth to do otherwise. Paradoxically, rather than reassuring the Catholic authorities – or the respectable majority of Spanish people – this show of conformity only fostered greater fear. Spanish society was haunted by the spectre of a secret enemy, following alien practices underground. Hence the constant anxiety about the presence of *Moriscos* in society's midst. These were people of Moorish origin who had (themselves or their forebears) been converted by force to Catholicism but whose loyalties lay with Islam underneath. The same went for Spain's *Marranos*. The word *marrano* (ironically, an Arabic one) had literally meant 'dirty' or 'unclean', in the ritual sense of being 'taboo' and so it came to mean a pig, which was forbidden both to Muslims and Jews. In early-modern Spain, it was used to refer to those Jews who (or whose ancestors), despite having officially converted to Catholicism, still followed Jewish practice secretly. The word was of course a deeply unpleasant swipe at the 'dirty', forbidden status of such Jews, but it was also a jibe at their own careful avoidance of pigs and pork.

THE INDEX

THE CATHOLIC CHURCH has always been at pains to stress its deep commitment to the cause of reason. It has always claimed that there's no incompatibility between science and religion. And in truth, in our own time, while American Protestant churches bang the drum for fundamentalism, successive Popes have expressed their belief in evolution. Oddly, it might be thought, Charles Darwin's *The Descent of Man* has never fallen foul of the Church's censors – even in the nineteenth century, when it first appeared.

This stance is still more surprising given the historical readiness of Catholic prelates to slap wholesale bans on books or authors. Their repressiveness is recorded in a handy checklist. The *Index* – or, to give it its full title, the *Index Librorum Prohibitorum* ('Index of Prohibited Books') – is a veritable catalogue of Catholic intolerance, and to most modern eyes a collective act of utter folly.

It's unsurprising, if perhaps a little unenlightened, that the theological works of famous Protestant reformers like Luther and Calvin should have been included – but what of an otherwise blameless botanist like Otto Braunfels? What makes a flower or leaf heretical? Did Konrad Gesner's Protestantism really vitiate all his zoological findings? Was his description of the guinea pig as threatening as the observations of Galileo? The latter was eventually removed from the *Index* by a sheepish Catholic establishment in 1741. No such luck for philosophers from Locke, Hobbes and Hume to Jean-Paul Sartre and Simone de Beauvoir. Also included are creative writers from John Milton to Honoré de Balzac and Graham Greene.

That Greene was a Catholic didn't save him: his offence seems to have been his specific slights against the priesthood. For far more obviously 'problematic' works have gone unnoticed by the Church's censors. Karl Marx's writings, for example, atheistic as they are, and D.H. Lawrence's racier scribblings: they may not be recommended reading but they weren't banned.

Opposite: Galileo fights his corner before the Italian Inquisition – notoriously, the hearing concluded with dogma defeating science. In this case at least – and only unconvincingly, and for the moment. In the long run, Catholicism's obdurate resistance to rational enquiry was to prove self-defeating.

authorities in Italy in the same way as it had in Spain and Portugal, and its scope for action was much more limited as a result.

It did nevertheless make a considerable contribution to Catholicism's history – and a disproportionate one to its 'dark history', it might be said. For the Church's unique role in defending superstition, in fighting a rearguard action against the advance of scientific understanding and rational intelligence, was spearheaded by the Roman Inquisition.

Take the example of Nicolaus Copernicus (1473–1543) – himself a Catholic cleric, and a naïve believer in the official line that the Church saw no incompatibility between religious faith and scientific reason. His book *De revolutionibus orbium coelestium* ('On the Revolutions of the Heavenly Spheres', 1543) was a revolution in itself. Rejecting the ancient assumption that the cosmos was 'geocentric' – centred around the Earth – it proposed that the Earth and planets orbited the sun in a 'heliocentric' system. Copernicus was slapped down by the Inquisition for his pains.

Galileo Galilei (1564–1642) took Copernicus' findings further, his observations of Venus and of Jupiter (with its 'Galilean Moons') all tending to confirm the earlier scientist's work. Notoriously, the 'Father of Modern Physics' was hauled up before the Inquisition in 1632 and forced to recant his 'heretical' theories under threat of torture. Having admitted that the Earth stood still, he reputedly muttered 'And yet it moves'.

Despite his show of obedience, Galileo was placed under house arrest – where he'd stay for the next ten years; it went without saying that his books were banned. Not just those he'd actually written, but any he might conceivably think about writing at some point in the future – the Inquisition seemed resolved to cast the Church in as ludicrous a light as possible.

VII

THE SPLENDOUR AND THE SQUALOR

The Renaissance saw the Catholic Church at the very zenith of its power and wealth, yet it seemed anything but spiritual at the top. Financial corruption, sexual license and the building of nepotistic dynasties: a triumphant papacy presided over an increasingly beleaguered Church.

◆

'Your riches have rotted and your garments are moth-eaten.' – *JAMES 5:2*

'Blessed are the meek,' Our Lord had said – but there was no sign of them inheriting the Earth just yet, and certainly not that corner of the Earth that housed the Holy See in Rome. Ruthless ambition and greed were more the order of the day down here – vast wealth, megalomaniac vanity and an arrogant contempt for the plight of the poor and the preoccupations of the lowly. This period in the Church's history has left a legacy of magnificence, it

Opposite: Giuliano de' Medici falls before the onslaught from the Pazzi. The outrage had been at least tacitly authorized by Pope Sixtus IV, it seemed. The Church's embracing of Renaissance realpolitik helped enhance its power and wealth immensely – but at enormous moral and spiritual cost.

can't be denied: clerical patronage underwrote much of that artistic and cultural achievement we now think of as the 'Renaissance'. But it also left a sense of ethical abandonment that Catholicism is still struggling to live down. What could so much wealth and pomp have to do with the spirit of the Gospels?

Murder in the Cathedral

Around 10,000 had gathered in the *duomo* for morning mass to celebrate the Resurrection of Christ Our Saviour from the dead. New life, human redemption and fresh spring after the lengthy winter of damnation – Easter was the highpoint of the Christian year. For a group of cruel conspirators, though, the day was marked out as one for murder: they had come to Florence's famous cathedral to assassinate Lorenzo de' Medici and his brother Giuliano. The Medici family had dominated the affairs of the Italian city for half a century; now their rivals, the Pazzi clan, were calling time.

FATHER... AND NEPHEW

THAT THE CATHOLIC Church is utterly obsessed with sex has been an article of faith with modern critics, and it isn't difficult to see why this should be. On the one hand, there have been the all but impossibly exacting standards set for the sexual conduct of lay Catholics; on the other, there've been the clergy's many (and varied) fallings short. So, amid all the fuss there's been about everything from gay marriage to contraception, it has been easy to forget that the Church has any other interests. Likewise, it's been easy to assume that the Church's longstanding insistence on clerical celibacy has stemmed from a feeling that Christ's ministers had to be sexually pure.

Historically, as it happens, that doesn't seem to have been the case. Clerical celibacy may indeed often have been justified in terms of the special status attributed to chastity, but this doesn't seem to have been the basis for the ideal. Rather, the intention seems to have been that priests shouldn't have extra-clerical emotional or (more important still) financial ties: they should be married to the Church, owing it not just their allegiance but any property they might have. They shouldn't be building dynastic families of their own or trying to leave accumulated wealth or possessions outside the Church.

In practice (at least in medieval practice) the absence of marital ties only opened the way to other, slightly wider, familial loyalties. The modern word 'nepotism' (from the Latin word *nepos*, meaning nephew) was first used to describe the policies of those popes who advanced their families by doing favours for the sons of their own brothers or sisters. Sixtus IV made no fewer than six of his nephews into cardinals. One – Giuliano della Rovere – was to become Pope Julius II. Not that his nieces were allowed to remain idle: they were strategically married into Italy's leading families. The network of Sixtus' connections stretched far and wide.

Heedless of hallowed ground and the presence of the Blessed Sacrament on the altar above them, a group of Pazzi thugs attacked the Medici benches, daggers drawn. As worshippers screamed and recoiled with fear, they surged forward, pushing past the Medici henchmen who came out to meet them, making determinedly for the two men they had come to kill. Giuliano fell beneath a rain of blows – stabbed 19 times in all, he was to bleed out in a matter of minutes on the cathedral floor. But his elder brother was only wounded in the shoulder. The fighting spilled out across the lobby, through the great doorway and into the streets outside: only now did the scale of the conspiracy become clear. In what amounted to a wholesale coup attempt, the Pazzi and their friends had tried to take charge of the Signoria – the seat of government – but they were beaten back by forces loyal to the Medici.

Opposite: Sixtus IV cuts a striking – if worldly – figure as befits a ruler declaring war. His conflict with the Medici ushered in a time of turbulence in Italy and in the Church at large, its worldly wealth the object now of envy and faction-fighting.

Bundled quickly out of danger's way, Lorenzo lived to restore order and resume his authority as the leading powerbroker in Florence and in Italy.

Dirty Work

What has gone down in history as the Pazzi Conspiracy of 1478 had been to a large extent the brainchild of the Pope. The Pazzi had been pawns. A crime combining murderous attack with the most outrageous sort of sacrilege had been committed on behalf of Catholicism's leader. The Salviati family, Sixtus IV's bankers and an old family with important connections in several cities – including both Florence and Rome – had helped to organize an attack intended to increase the influence of Francesco Salviati, Archbishop of Pisa, by promoting Pope Sixtus' power at the expense of the Medicis.

We're a long way here from the spirit of loving thy neighbour, embracing poverty and turning the other cheek to oppression. Niccolò Machiavelli, a Medici protégé and the notorious apologist for this sort of ruthless *realpolitik*, had yet to write his revolutionary

Opposite: As famously portrayed by Raphael, Pope Julius II was a formidable – even threatening – figure, but the 'Warrior Pope' won his place by nepotism. Sixtus IV had been his uncle: while popes couldn't father children (officially, at least), even so they were able to establish dynasties.

treatise *Il Principe* ('The Prince', 1532). But if his thinking had not been formulated, its spirit was already alive and flourishing in a Florence – and an Italy – in which power was always up for grabs. The winner might take all, but no one expected to be the winner by pulling his political punches, by flinching from violence or resisting corruption of any kind.

All in the Family

Sixtus' sister, Bianca della Revere, had married Paolo Riario, the powerful lord of Imola, north of Florence and near Bologna. Their son, Girolamo, grew up to be his uncle's favourite, and was appointed 'Captain General' – commander of the papal army. This should have been an oxymoronic position, it might be thought,

but the Papal States were territories that had to be defended like any other. As a temporal ruler, the Pope also had to have a 'foreign policy'. This was placed under the supervision of another of Sixtus' nephews, Pietro della Revere. Girolamo's marriage into the family of the Dukes of Milan had meanwhile given him extensive lands in north and central Italy. This in turn had fostered the ambition of building even greater power in the country. The Medici family were the main obstacle in his way, hence his alliance with the Pazzi, their local rivals.

The failure of the Pazzi Conspiracy left both sides badly weakened. For Girolamo and Sixtus there was severe loss of face. For the Pazzi there was a decade of harassment, eased only by the comparative weakness of the Medici family given that Florence had been subjected to what amounted to a spiritual embargo by the Pope. On Sixtus' orders, the saying of the mass and the consecration of the Eucharist were outlawed in the city. A deeply vindictive action when it is considered that most of those in Florence had played no part in

FAIR-WEATHER FRIEND?

SEVENTEENTH-CENTURY ENGLISH HISTORIAN John Bale insisted that Sixtus IV gave his cardinals 'the authorization to commit sodomy during periods of warm weather'. Bale, it has to be acknowledged, was a Protestant pamphleteer – hardly the most independent of sources on papal history. A certain scepticism is also needed when approaching the contemporary diary of Stefano Infessura, who repeatedly refers to Sixtus as a sodomite and says that he handed out Church offices in return for sexual favours. Sixtus' own nephew Pietro was a major beneficiary, he claims. Infessura was a republican and a political enemy of the Pope – but what are we to make of similar testimony by the Venetian ambassador of the time, and the Pope's own master of ceremonies, Johann Burchard?

Right: John 'Bilious' Bale was known for his ill-temper, but he reserved his most bitter feeling for the Church of Rome. Disillusioned, he threw in his lot with Henry VIII's Reformation, for which his writings became a powerful propaganda tool.

THE PORNOGRAPHER POPE

BEFORE HE BECAME Pope Pius II in 1458 – before he'd even established himself as a priest, indeed – Eneas Silvius Piccolomini had a reputation as a writer. Not quite on a par with Virgil, the Roman poet to whose epic hero his first name made clear reference – and whose standard description *Pius Aeneas* ('pious' or 'dutiful' Aeneas) his papal name acknowledges.

He *was* a writer and scholar, although, even if some of his wisdom seems strange in a man of God: his 'moral' treatise *The Institution of the Nobleman*

recommends that its readers find an outlet for sexual frustration in extramarital affairs, for instance.

His subsequent novel, *Historia de Duobus Amantibus* ('A Tale of Two Lovers') concerned two characters who decided to do just that, one Euryalus and a married lover named Lucretia.

AN 'EPISTOLARY' NOVEL in the sense that its text takes the form of the two lovers' letters, it was frankly erotic in its subject matter – and a best-seller across fifteenth century Europe.

recent events, yet they were being deprived of those sacraments they hoped would save their souls.

Popetown

While not, presumably, stinting in his efforts on behalf of what Augustine had called the City of God, Pius II also built a city of his own. Pienza, as he called it, was in fact a wholesale redevelopment of the village of Corsignano, Tuscany, in which he himself had been born in 1405. He saw it as a summer retreat, but also as an expression of the highest principles of Renaissance planning and architecture. The streets and squares were laid out with wonderful regularity, the houses handsome and the *palazzi* splendid – it was pretty much a condition of getting a cardinalship from Pius that you agreed to build a palace in Pienza. There have been many much graver papal crimes, of course – indeed, Pius II did posterity an enormous favour in founding and constructing his model city. But it was an enormous work of vanity, nonetheless.

Not So Innocent

Not for Giovanni Battista Cibò, from 1484 Pope Innocent VIII, the cynical nepotism of his predecessors. Granted, he had secured his position through the good offices of Guiliano della Rovere, nephew of Sixtus IV's nephew (and future Pope Julius II). But Innocent was above such dealings. Why give lands, titles and properties to nephews, after all, when you've begotten two sons of your very own? Some sources suggest a great many more – as many as a hundred, it has been

suggested, although Reformation satirists could be quite extravagant in their claims.

Innocent's approach to the question of clerical celibacy is summed up in an incident reported by Stefano Infessura. One of the Pope's most senior officials, says the diarist:

'Watchful of his flock as befits an honourable man, published an edict forbidding clergy as well as laics, whatever their position might be, from keeping

---

Indeed, such lives did the clergy lead that there was scarcely a single priest who did not have his mistress.

---

mistresses, whether openly or secretly... When the Pope heard this, he summoned his Vicar and ordered him immediately to cancel his command, saying that the practice was not in fact forbidden. Indeed, such lives did the clergy lead that there was scarcely a single priest who did not have his mistress. The number of prostitutes living in Rome at that time came to 6800 – not counting those who plied their trade under the

Opposite: Seen here as an old man, Pope Pius II had in his youth been more raffish than reverent: an intellectual, a poet, a writer of erotic fiction. A true 'Renaissance Man', his interests were wide-ranging and extended from religion to town planning.

PIVS·PAPA·II·SENENSIS·

Above: If Pius II had never achieved anything else, he would have been of interest as builder of Pienza, a real jewel of a Tuscan town. Carefully conceived and lovingly laid out, it fulfilled all the principles of Renaissance planning. This view shows the Palazzo Comunale or town hall.

guise of housekeepers or otherwise in secret.'

That said, the two sons of Innocent we know of for certain had both been born before Cibò had been in holy orders – a fairly trivial transgression, then, by the standards of the day. Far more serious was the extent to which *Il Papa* ('the Pope') pulled all the strings he could to secure his sons' advancement in society, in politics and the Church.

The elder, Franceschetto, a spoilt child, grew up to be a wastrel and an arrogant bully. Late into the night, he would strut about the streets of Rome with his rowdy friends. 'He forced his way into the houses of the citizens for evil purposes', one contemporary reported. His gambling habit was legendary – but, unfortunately for his family, completely true: once he contrived to lose 14,000 ducats in a single night at cards. So broke was he that, taking advantage of his father's final illness, he tried to take the entire papal treasury for himself. On Innocent's death, finding himself with no protector to look out for him, Franceschetto had to flee from Rome. Even so, Franceschetto had – by Innocent's good offices – married well. He had indeed wedded into the Medici family. Putting the Pazzi Conspiracy behind them, Florence's first family had continued to accumulate power, becoming a major force in Italy as a whole.

Borgia Beginnings

Right now, though, another clan was coming to the fore in Church affairs: the Borgias were descendants of the Spanish House of Borja. The first of the notorious 'Borgia Popes', Callixtus III (in office 1455–58) had actually conducted himself fairly blamelessly. His consuming preoccupation, apart from prayer and worship, had been the attempt to organize a crusade to recover Constantinople from the Ottoman Turks. That this came to nothing was down to quixotic incompetence rather than to malice or corruption. Callixtus could have been a great deal worse, historians concur. He was, it's true, a tireless promoter of his nephews' interests – but nepotism was the norm now, as we have seen. Callixtus would have been all but forgotten had it not been for one nephew in particular: created a cardinal by his uncle, Rodrigo Borgia became Pope on the death of Innocent VIII in 1492. Taking the title Alexander VI, he was to reign as St Peter's heir for 11 years.

Mixed Signals on Slavery

The year of 1492 was Alexander VI's accession, but it is of course more famous for Columbus' discovery of the Americas. It was also the year in which the Muslim Moors were finally driven out of Spain. Between the culture of crusade that had prevailed in previous centuries, and the new sense of opportunity opening up with the Age of Discovery, there was much soul-searching about the rights and wrongs of owning slaves.

Surprisingly, perhaps, Christ himself has nothing to say on the subject in the Gospels – although the Old Testament takes slavery as a given. The Church's

attitudes had changed, veering back and forth between unreflecting acceptance and bland discouragement, but there was no apparent feeling that the institution was *ipso facto* wrong. Rather, a consensus emerged that, while the enslavement of Christians was self-evidently an outrage and the enslavement of *anyone* less than ideal, in one case slavery could be justified. If it brought a benighted Pagan into contact with the one true faith, then a great right was bundled up in a small wrong.

The first forays by Portuguese navigators down the western side of Africa found whole nations of heathens excluded from God's grace (and conveniently only lightly-armed); soon seafarers were opening up new countries over the Atlantic. As the native population

Right: A picture of piety, it would appear – but Innocent VIII was so far from living up to his name that, by some accounts, he had fathered a hundred children. The Renaissance papacy was more a worldly than a spiritual position, and successive popes conducted themselves just like temporal rulers.

INNOCENTIVS ·VIII· PAPA·GENVENSIS ·
fu fatto del 1484 uise ani 7 messi o giorni 11

We grant ... full and unhindered licence to attack, seek out, take captive and make conquest of the Saracens and Pagans ...

plummeted, felled by unfamiliar Old World infections or worked to death by their Christian conquerors, the solution became apparent: ship the first group to the Americas to replace the second.

The Church's role in what was to become the Atlantic slave trade was strictly secondary: no Pope or prelate told the traders that this was what they had

to do. As the age's supposed moral arbiter, though, the Church was looked to for 'permission' – and this, there is no doubt, it freely gave. Tacitly, for the most part, but to some extent – just sufficiently – its approval was expressed, most notably in Pope Nicholas V's bull or pronouncement *Dum Diversas*. The meaning of the Latin title (basically, 'till things are different') suggests the interim nature of the statement – but it was to cover the lifetimes of many millions, to their tragic cost.

'We grant', it said, the Kings of Spain and Portugal – the two great Catholic powers driving the new colonialism, 'full and unhindered licence to attack, seek out, take captive and make conquest of the Saracens and Pagans, as well as any other infidels and foes of

Opposite: Alexander VI has been widely regarded as the ultimate 'Renaissance Pope' – with all that implies in the way of rapacity and ruthlessness. Though actually the second of the 'Borgia Popes', he's the one who shaped the dynasty's reputation for libertinism and murder on an epic scale.

Below: The King of the Congo receives Portuguese soldiers as three Christian missionaries stand beside the King in this illustration showing Portugal's sixteenth-century colonisation of the Congo. Christianity gained a quick hold in central Africa, with churches being built throughout the region.

Christ, wherever they may be found, along with their kingdoms, duchies, counties, principalities and other properties … and to take them into perpetual slavery.'

Alexander the Terrible

The very idea of the 'Renaissance Pope' conjures up an impression of power, opulence and corruption gone entirely mad, an outrageous cocktail of magnificence and sleaze. And the ultimate Renaissance Pope – the

one against all others were measured (and by whose reputation all have been to some extent smeared) was an effective – even conscientious – administrator of the Church, it seems. It was in everything else that Alexander fell short – in his sexual practices and his murderous politicking; and in what's generally considered to have been one of the most profoundly corrupt and cynical of papal reigns. After, all Rome was saying, 'buying' the conclave that elected him, setting

Below: If Christ could forgive Mary Magdalen, Alexander VI could go one (or forty-nine) better, celebrating his daughter Lucrezia's marriage by entertaining fifty courtesans in the Vatican. Notorious in every way, Alexander wasn't so much a legend in his own lifetime as a one-man argument for Reformation.

Opposite: Pope Alexander VI, his family and followers find financial redemption in Jesus' sacrifice: the Borgias saw Christ's Church as a treasure to be plundered. Alexander came to embody everything that was wrong with Catholicism. His papacy brought the Church into its greatest-ever disrepute.

up cooperative cardinals in sumptuous palaces at his own expense, he quickly made it clear that he saw the Church of Christ as a source of cash. Not just for himself but for his family. As his contemporary Gian Andrea Boccaccio put it in a letter to his friend, the Duke of Ferrara, 'ten papacies would not be enough to satisfy his kinsfolk'.

> ... these virtues were bound up with still greater faults: his manner of living was dissolute, and he knew neither shame nor sincerity, neither faith nor religion.

Rodrigo had started as he'd meant to go on, the riotous dissoluteness of his life unaffected by his anointment as a cardinal at the age of 29. Pope Pius II had reason to feel embarrassment almost immediately, as he explained in a letter:

'Four days ago, a number of ladies of Siena who are completely given up to worldly frivolities were gathered in the gardens of Giovanni di Bichis. We have been told that you, without heed to the high office you are invested with, remained in their company from the seventeenth hour to the twenty-second ... From what we hear, the most licentious dances were performed; no amorous activities went unpractised; while you yourself conducted yourself in an entirely worldly and unclerical manner. Decorum prevents my stating all that is said to have taken place, since not only the acts but their very names are unworthy of one in your position.'

A Wolf in Shepherd's Clothing

If he had been solely a sexual predator, Rodrigo's reputation wouldn't now be anything like so bad, but his enemies feared him as a murderous Machiavel, a cunning schemer. The young Giovanni de' Medici knew well what to expect of his appointment, observing to another cardinal, 'Now we are in the

Opposite: Lucrezia Borgia, beautiful and dangerous, looks slyly sidelong from Bartolomeo Veneto's portrait. The daughter of a 'celibate' pope, Lucrezia would have been an ironic comment on the state of the Church even if she hadn't gone on to have incestuous relations with her brother and her (holy) father.

power of a wolf, the most rapacious, perhaps, that this world has ever seen; and, if we do not flee, he will infallibly devour us.'

A (perhaps) more fair-minded judgement comes from the Florentine historian and statesman Guicciardini (1483–1540). 'Alexander', he writes, 'was very active, and possessed of remarkable penetration; his judgment was excellent, and he had a wonderful power of persuasion; in all serious business he displayed an incredible attention and ability.'

'But' – and there was bound to be a 'but', of course: 'these virtues were bound up with still greater faults: his manner of living was dissolute, and he knew neither shame nor sincerity, neither faith nor religion.'

A damning judgement on the head of any major creed, it might be thought, but Guicciardini isn't done, continuing: 'He, moreover, was possessed by an insatiable greed, an overwhelming ambition, a more than barbarous cruelty, and a burning passion for the advancement of his many children, who, in order to carry out his iniquitous decrees, did not scruple to employ the most heinous means.'

If Alexander had a redeeming feature, it was perhaps his outrageous freedom from hypocrisy: he flaunted his mistresses and openly doted on his children. Nine have been identified for certain, although there may well have been many more. The first of his publicly acknowledged mistresses, Giovanna ('Vannozza') dei Cattanei, bore him four children: Giovanni, Cesare, Lucrezia and Gioffre. Of these, the first became Duke of Gandia when he grew up; the second the Duke of Valentinois; and Lucrezia, at one time or another, the Duchess variously of Ferrara, Modena and Reggio.

Lovely Lucrezia

Lucrezia was the most controversial woman of her age. Between three marriages and rumoured affairs (two of them incestuous, with her father and her brother, Cesare), she's been remembered as the ultimate Machiavellian she-devil. Bewitching with her beauty; seducing with her smile; pouring poison into her victims' drinks from a hollow ring...

Where history meets myth is hard to say so many centuries on. Another side to the *femme fatale* emerges in Florentine Ambassador Lorenzo Pucci's account of a visit to Lucrezia in her palazzo on Christmas Eve 1493. He found Alexander's latest mistress, Giulia Farnese –

PRETTY AS A PICTURE

VANNOZZA DEI CATTANEI may have been the most enduring, but of all Alexander's mistresses it is Giulia della Farnese we feel we know the best. We can actually see her face in several major works of Renaissance art. 'Giulia la Bella' – Julia the Beautiful – her contemporaries called her, and it isn't difficult to understand why when we see her in Pinturicchio's depiction of the Madonna and Child, with Pope Alexander kneeling at her feet.

Or rather, of surviving copies, for the fresco was subsequently lost – perhaps destroyed, given the obvious indecorousness of an image of this kind. Was Alexander laughing at everyone? It's hard to get inside the head of a man who, on the one hand, seems to have treated his sacred position with such cavalier contempt, but to have been a reasonably serious official of the Church in other ways. Likewise, we can't help wondering whether there wasn't an element of satire in Giulia's depiction (completely nude), as the allegorical figure of Justice before the tomb of her brother Alessandro, who reigned as Pope Paul III from 1534 to 1549. She remained quite naked till the mid-nineteenth century, when a scandalized Pope Leo IX had a metal chemise made for her and painted it white to match the marble.

Best of Enemies

Pope Pius III, Alexander's successor, was the son of Pius II's sister. His sickness and death, after a reign of only 26 days, inevitably sparked suggestions of foul play – perhaps of poisoning. He was followed on to St Peter's throne by Pope Julius II – no one's nephew, for a change, but great-nephew of Sixtus IV. In keeping with the clerical mores of the age, he had an illegitimate daughter. Felice della Rovere was destined to become a major player in the politics of the time. There were also some who said his friendship with the handsome young Cardinal Francesco Alidosi was closer than perhaps

and their daughter, Laura – living with Lucrezia quite happily:

'I called at the house of Santa Maria in Portico to see Madonna Giulia. She had just finished washing her hair when I entered, and was sitting by the fire with Madonna Lucrezia, the daughter of our Master, and Madonna Adriana, who all received me with every appearance of pleasure. Madonna Giulia asked me to sit by her side … Giulia also wanted me to see the child; she is now quite big, and it seems to me, resembles the Pope…'

The greetings over, the company all trooped through together to hear mass, after which the Ambassador made his farewells – leaving this little blended family behind, a picture of domestic bliss.

it should have been. He certainly seems to have over-promoted his protégé, placing him in charge of a papal army he wasn't remotely competent to command – and then to have been broken-hearted when he was murdered by the angry general who'd been forced to take the blame.

A rival of Alexander in 1492, Julius had been incensed by his election – so much so that he'd gone stomping off to France. There he'd stirred up King Charles VIII with stories of sharp practice by princes and cardinals – to such effect that the French King had launched an invasion of the Kingdom of Naples. Julius

came along for the ride – and for Rome, of course – but to no avail: Alexander had outmanoeuvred him, making his own deal with King Charles' chief minister.

Ultimately – and anticlimactically – Julius won the papacy without really trying. Alexander died in 1503, by which time his son Cesare was sick himself. Any idea that he'd become the next Borgia Pope had to be

Below: Charles VIII entering Florence in 1494, as imagined by artist Giuseppe Bezzuoli (1784–1855). Charles invaded Italy with 25,000 men in 1494. He marched across the peninsula, subduing Florence on the way, and reached Naples in February 1495.

FORZA FELICE!

BORN OF HER father's long-term liaison with
Lucrezia Normanni, an aristocratic Roman
widow, Felice della Rovere was brought up within
the institution of the Church. Marrying into the
rich and powerful Orsini family, she became one
of Italy's most influential women, a major force
in the politics of the day. Less colourful than
Lucrezia Borgia, she was arguably much more
important, a major power behind the papal throne
– not just her father's, but those of his successors
Leo X and Clement VII. The feminine force who
really drove this seemingly most patriarchal of
institutions, Felice was the nearest there's ever
been to a Pope Joan.

dropped abruptly at this point, and so it was that Julius
was duly crowned.

His reign continued quietly: indeed, Julius is now
generally best remembered for being the man who
commissioned Michelangelo to paint the ceiling of
the Sistine Chapel. Was the great artist just the latest
in a series of male favourites? Was there – at very least
– an erotic undertone to their relationship? That has
certainly been suggested, and it might help explain the
tempestuousness of the Pope and painter's dealings
down the years.

'Let Us Enjoy It'

The year of 1513 saw the final emergence of the
Medici on to the wider Italian stage with the election
of Giovanni di Lorenzo de' Medici as Pope Leo X. A
crucial breakthrough for the family, and one that had
been a long time coming. That said, there's a danger in
seeing the Church politics of this time as too much in
terms of dynastic struggle. Leo wasn't just his family's
representative in Rome, he was his own man – and that

Left: Pinturicchio's famous fresco, painted in the Duomo or cathedral
of Siena in 1500–01 captures the pomp and splendour of the
Renaissance papacy. Here Pius III is crowned, a powerful temporal as
well as a spiritual leader, attended by his bishops, his Swiss Guard –
and a cheering crowd.

man was, in his way, not unappealing. 'Since God has given us the papacy,' he said, 'let us enjoy it.'

And so he did, with a spendthrift determination that smacked of fanaticism, entertaining continuously on the most lavish scale. It wasn't just that he gave good parties (although his banquets were legendary, the sumptuous food and wine equalled by the spectacular shows of music and dancing), he also sponsored cultural events and popular parades. As well as a patron of the Arts (most famously Raphael), he also made lavish endowments to science and scholarship. An unabashed highbrow, Leo at the same time wasn't too uptight for lower entertainments: he loved broad clowning, and even had his own personal buffoon, Fra Mariano Fetti, employed at a stipend of 800 ducats a year. His vulgar taste for curiosities came together with his connoisseurship in strange examples of 'higher whimsy' – like the portrait of his pet elephant Hanno he commissioned from Raphael.

Above: Pope Julius II kneels as, at the miraculous Mass of Bolsena (shown here by Raphael), the consecrated host begins to bleed. Just visible behind the last of the candle-bearers – dark-haired, in dark clothes and with her head just tilted – his daughter, Felice, directs operations from the rear.

Leo was also enthusiastic for architecture. He had old churches restored and new ones built. The construction of the New St Peter's, set in motion by Nicholas V, then continued in expanded form under Julius II, really began to gather pace under his papacy.

It would be quite wrong to assume that, despite these expensive tastes, Leo lived entirely for himself. His generosity was impressive – excessive, even. Hospitals, orphanages, convents, the poor: all were to receive substantial help. Christ himself couldn't have found him wanting as far as open-handedness was concerned. The big problem was going to be paying for it all.

THE PRISONER OF CASTEL SANT'ANGELO

THERE HAD BEEN far worse Popes than Leo X, but few who'd been so frankly worldly. The Renaissance had swept away any sense of the Pontiff as primarily a spiritual leader. Popes were powerful potentates now – but, oddly, this had the effect of making them more vulnerable, exposed as they were to all the turbulence of Earthly politics and diplomacy. Their presence as 'players' in the international arena meant that they were no longer seen as untouchable by worldly rulers, as the second Medici Pope, Clement VII, was to find. The alliance he'd made with France's Francis I to gain leverage against the Holy Roman Emperor Charles V irritated that impatient ruler beyond endurance. In 1527, accordingly, he invaded Italy and the papal army was badly defeated. In the event, though, both Pope

and Emperor got more than they had bargained for in the battle's aftermath when mutinous Imperial forces ran amok. The Sack of Rome, although a clear defeat for the papacy, could hardly be described as a victory for the Emperor, who looked on in helpless horror as his soldiers raped and plundered in the city. Clement spent six months imprisoned inside his own summer residence, Castel Sant'Angelo, and had to pay his captors a substantial bribe for his release.

Below: The Sack of Rome, 1527, was a devastating blow to the Eternal City, an embarrassment for Charles V, but an insurmountable humiliation for the Papacy. The Holy Father Clement VII, held prisoner in the Castel Sant'Angelo, had to pay a substantial ransom for his release.

VIII

FROM REFORMATION TO ENLIGHTENMENT

The Renaissance party left an acrid hangover, the sins of centuries catching up with a Church that had exhausted its credit – financially and spiritually. Faith gave way to cynicism: reformers found new ways of following Christ, while philosophers questioned the foundations of belief.

'The true light, which enlightens everyone ...'   — *JOHN 1: 9*

Leo left a legacy of unrivalled splendour, and Western art is forever in his debt. But his spiritual contribution is harder to detect. And, while he doesn't seem to have been personally immoral on the scale of so many of his predecessors (vague rumours of the odd gay relationship aside), his outrageous spending brought the Church to near-ruin – complete and utter ruin, some would say. Some did, indeed, most notably Martin Luther, the German priest whose indignation was to bring about a Reformation.

Opposite: Martin Luther burns the bull with which Pope Leo X had attempted to refute his charges. The Reformation released a surge of theological passion and intellectual energy – but also a wave of violent intolerance.

The Pawnshop Pope

It has to be admitted that, in his desperation to fund his spending, Leo was resourceful, and he didn't stand pompously upon the dignity of the Church. After all, what previous Pope had tried to replenish his dwindling coffers by calling in the pawnbrokers to carry off artworks and furnishings from the great churches and papal palaces? Where Christ had angrily driven the moneylenders from the Temple, his successor, it seemed, was eagerly inviting them in. But this financial catastrophe was nothing to the moral and spiritual bankruptcy that was now to beset the Church.

Julius II's plan for a new St Peter's, calling as it did on vast reserves of funding, had sent the Church's campaign for donations into overdrive. A rebuilt basilica had first been mooted by Pope Nicholas V in the fifteenth century, but Julius II redrafted his proposals on a far bigger scale. A cynic might suggest that he conceived of the vast new basilica as a fitting

house for the imposing tomb he'd commissioned for himself, rather than for the bones of St Peter or as a spiritual headquarters for his Church. Leo X took up Julius' project with his customary enthusiasm and, as

---

Desiderius Erasmus, the Dutch humanist, wrote of the disgraceful 'degeneracy' of priests who were actually 'filthy, ignorant, impudent vagabonds'.

---

his vision expanded, so did the expense. The Pope's solution, elegant in its simplicity, was calamitous in its implications. Not content with pawning material luxuries, he started pawning his powers of pardoning, selling indulgences in frank and unquestioning exchange for cash. The system, as we've seen had always been open to abuse: now the Pope had opened up a market in divine forgiveness.

A Crisis of Confidence

Conscientious Catholics couldn't help but be aware of the flaws of the Church and its hierarchy. For the most part, though, they managed to forgive them. Even if the institution was human, the faith was divine, they'd reasoned: the office was greater than the man and the Church much bigger than its clergy.

Desiderius Erasmus, the Dutch humanist, spoke for many when he wrote of the 'universally acknowledged' corruption of the Holy See, and the disgraceful 'degeneracy' of priests who, while claiming to be like the Apostles, were actually 'filthy, ignorant, impudent vagabonds'. They pretended to poverty but in reality wormed their way into men's homes and polluted them with evil: 'Wasps that they are, no one dares exclude them for fear of their stings.' Even so, Erasmus remained loyal to the Church. Others, though, their confidence crumbling, began to wonder whether Catholicism could still be justified, even in theological terms. The sale of indulgences may have been the last

Opposite: Pope Julius II climbs up to inspect Michelangelo's ongoing work on the ceiling of the Sistine Chapel. The relationship between the painter and his patron were notoriously fraught, but the result was one of the most spectacular artistic achievements of all time.

spiritual straw for theologian Martin Luther, but his disillusion had gone a great deal further by the time he made his stand of 1517. It is impossible to know in hindsight how far ethical disgust prompted spiritual questioning, but it certainly created a context in which the unthinkable could be thought. John Calvin's theological break with Rome ended up extending far beyond the corruption issue, but his rebellion was clearly given impetus by his moral outrage. For him, the trade in relics didn't just seem distasteful, it discredited Catholicism. If all the relics in the world were brought together, he suggested, 'it would be made manifest that every Apostle has more than four bodies, and every Saint two or three.' In other words, the sins of the Church weren't just tarnishing its reputation, they were undermining the very basis of belief.

BROUGHT TO BOOK

WHAT BECAME KNOWN as 'Protestantism' grew out of intellectual questioning, not just moral disdain. The Renaissance had brought a ferment of ideas, and printing technology had distributed the benefits far and wide. A growing middle class felt more self-confident and secure in every area of life, especially in the prosperous cities of northern Europe. Why not question religion too? Rather than tamely submit to being spoon-fed spiritual doctrine by their clergy, they expected to judge things for themselves. Whether consciously or subconsciously, Martin Luther had understood the new importance of the individual conscience in a way the Catholic hierarchy had yet to. In 1522, he published his German translation of the New Testament so that his parishioners could read the Gospels for themselves. William Tyndale's English Bible came out in 1525 to bitter condemnation from the Church. As Henry VIII's Lord Chancellor, St Thomas More was to have the works of both men burned. Tyndale himself was to suffer the same fate when he was caught by the Catholic authorities in Antwerp, Belgium, and condemned as a heretic: he went to the stake in 1536.

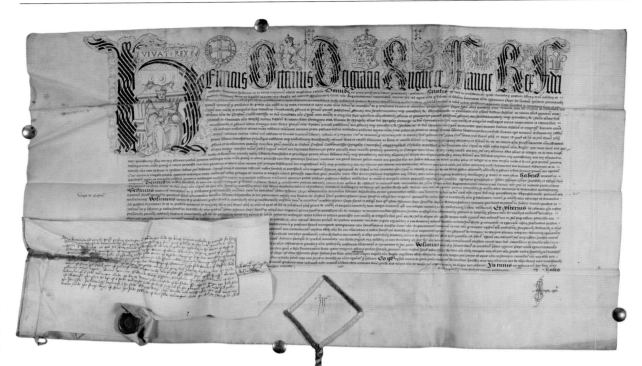

Above: Henry VIII's great seal authenticates the grant (to the ironically-named Sir Thomas Pope) of the lands and properties of the abbeys at Winchcombe, Battle and Bruerne. The English king saw the monasteries as an asset to be stripped systematically, to enrich himself and reward his faithful supporters.

About-turn in England

To this day, British coins carry the name of the reigning monarch, then the letters 'F.D.', which stands for *Fidei Defensor* – 'Defender of the Faith'. Leo X awarded this honorific to England's Henry VIII in recognition of his services to Catholicism. In 1521 the King (a considerable scholar) had published his own pamphlet, *A Defence of the Seven Sacraments* (1521), painstakingly dismantling many of Luther's objections to Church teaching. But when his Queen, Catherine of Aragon, proved unable to bear him a male heir, Henry found himself in conflict with the Holy See. When Pope Clement VII refused him the annulment of their marriage that would allow him to wed Anne Boleyn, Henry was enraged. From now on, he insisted, the monarch would be the head of England's Church.

Henry's theological thinking hadn't changed. His 'Church of England' was still Catholic in everything but its fealty to Rome. Protestant reform was actively discouraged – at least at first. Henry's main priorities were the centralization of his rule and the satisfaction of his ongoing need for funds. The 'Dissolution of the Monasteries', which got under way in 1536, was a means of furthering both these aims at once. The break-up of the monastic system allowed the King to confiscate lands and treasures, while at the same time destroying the power of the Catholic Church in the country at large. Everything from gold vessels and embroidered vestments to lead roof lining and wood were carted off from the monasteries, while local profiteers followed, raiding the ruins for building-stone.

As time went on, though, the Church of England started heading off in a more continental-style, Protestant direction. Henry's chief minister Thomas Cromwell and Archbishop of Canterbury Thomas Cranmer both had sympathies with some of Luther's reforming views. There was also a growing sense that 'Anglicanism' had to be marked out more theologically

Opposite: Henry confides in his trusted chancellor. Till his eventual disgrace and death in 1530, Thomas Wolsey would have given a Renaissance Pope a run for his money with the wealth and splendour of his lifestyle, and the immensity of his power.

A TALE OF THREE THOMASES

DICTATORIAL THOUGH HE may have been by nature, Henry's instinct was always to delegate. He ruled through a succession of ministers and Lord Chancellors – all named Thomas. The first one, Wolsey, was a cardinal of the Catholic Church, but was much more worldly in his focus as Lord Chancellor. His taxation reforms enriched the Crown even as his reforms to the justice system bolstered royal authority at the expense of local lords'. Wolsey's wealth and power became so great he was almost able to set himself up as a second King – a risky strategy when No.1 was so possessive of his prestige. The Cardinal's great palace at Hampton Court was confiscated by the King after Wolsey's inevitable fall from grace. (He faced treason charges when he sickened and died in 1530.) Wolsey's successor Thomas More has since been canonised by the Catholic Church to which he

did indeed stay loyal and for which, in 1535, he died a martyr's death. But he wasn't to be mourned by England's Protestants, of whom he'd proven a cruel persecutor. Several 'heretics' were burned at the stake during his reign. Thomas Cromwell was as cruel in his conviction as his predecessor had been, but the victims now were Catholics – holdouts against Henry's Reformation. For what it's worth, the new minister seems to have been sincere. In the end his Protestant reforming zeal so far outstripped the King's that he was taken prisoner and beheaded in the Tower in 1540.

Below: Antoine Caron's interest in classical antiquity comes out unexpectedly in his 1591 treatment of the arrest of Sir Thomas More. King Henry VIII appears (in the archway at left, on horseback) in more contemporary garb, but he was actually as tyrannical as any Roman emperor.

Above: Under Mary I, the English Reformation was thrown violently into reverse. These six Protestant martyrs were burned together in Canterbury in 1555. Such public shows may have served as a warning, but – whichever side conducted them – they also inspired with courage those quietly keeping up their faiths.

from what it was replacing: successive official prayer books pushed more Protestant doctrinal lines. Even now, though, the King set strict limits on religious faith: Henry VIII may have had some 60 Catholic martyrs executed, but more than 20 men and women were burned for preaching Protestant beliefs.

Henry had to have his kingdom run just-so. His consuming pathology was no more religious fanaticism than it was sex addiction. It was his ruthless, obsessively centralizing and controlling zeal.

Turn and Turn About

Henry's young son, Edward VI, succeeded his father when he died in 1547. Mature for his years, he seems to have thought deeply about his faith and brought real Protestant conviction to his reign. But it was over in the blink of an eye. Always sickly, Edward died in 1553. It

was all-change with the accession of Mary I. Henry's daughter didn't share his religious views. Hardly surprising, given that the Church of England had been brought into being specifically so her father could set aside her mother, Catherine of Aragon, who in her eyes had remained the rightful Queen of a Catholic England. 'Bloody Mary' was resolved to restore the One True Faith.

In furtherance of that cause an estimated 280 martyrs were burned at the stake – hundreds more were imprisoned and tortured by her agents.

Opposite: A woman writhes, hung in chains from a crane in a crowded street during an eruption of violence against France's seventeenth-century Protestants, or Huguenots. Such outrages were quietly condoned by a Crown and Catholic Church which had no wish to see the order of centuries overturned.

And all for nothing. Mary died in 1558, only for her half-sister Elizabeth I to take the throne. Now the Catholics were the martyrs once again. Elizabeth passed 'Penal Laws' preventing Catholics from holding public office or owning property. 'Recusants' – those who refused to swear their allegiance to Anglicanism – were hunted down. Catholic priests slipped into England secretly to help keep the creed alive in remote areas like Lancashire and Norfolk. Guerrilla-missionaries, they worked heroically underground. The country houses of Catholic families were equipped with special secret chapels and hiding-holes for priests, cunningly concealed in roof-spaces, under floors or behind false walls.

Sectarian Struggles

The Reformation polarized things. In those countries that continued to be Catholic, the Church became even more powerful than before. Catholic monarchs could see how easily the spiritual self-reliance the Protestants preached might be carried over into the sphere of worldly politics. In the Spanish Netherlands there could be no doubt: religious Reformation had brought calls for wider reforms and the Dutch had mobilized for independence. While the Inquisition redoubled its efforts here and in Spain, the French Crown cracked down hard on the Huguenots. Urged on by his queen – Mary, Queen of Scots – Francis II devoted his brief reign (1559–60) to the persecution of the Huguenots.

The decades that followed brought what have come to be known as the 'French Wars of Religion' as rival Catholic and Protestant factions fought it out. Or,

> The country houses of Catholic families were equipped with special hiding-holes for priests, cunningly concealed in roof-spaces, under floors or behind false walls.

rather, it might be said, the great aristocratic houses of Guise and Bourbon vied for supremacy – for the contest was clearly as much a dynastic as it was a religious one. There's no doubt, though, that – as was to happen in many other conflicts in the centuries that followed – familial and ideological tensions took on a religious aspect.

So it was to prove in the home of the Reformation. Germany was then a patchwork of smaller states, principalities and duchies divided along religious lines. Conflict had been averted earlier with the agreement at the Peace of Augsburg (1555) of the principle *cuius regio, cuius religio* ('whose region, whose religion'). In other words, if a ruler was Catholic, then that was the

THE ST BARTHOLOMEW'S DAY MASSACRE

THE MARRIAGE OF Henri III of Navarre to Charles IX's sister, Marguerite of Valois, in 1572 was meant to bring the two religious camps together: Henri was a Huguenot, Marguerite a Catholic. Unfortunately, many Catholics (not excluding the bride herself, it was rumoured) were bitterly opposed to the match. The Duke of Guise, the self-appointed leader of France's Catholic conservatives, was positively enraged. It didn't help that the Huguenot Admiral de Coligny was among the wedding guests: he was widely believed to have ordered the assassination of Guise's father years before. The attempt by one of Guise's men to get revenge by shooting Coligny ended in failure, but set the sectarian temperature in Paris soaring. Pre-empting any Huguenot reprisals, the Duke of Guise and his men followed up the first attack: bursting into Coligny's house, they quickly killed him. In the three days that followed, Catholic mobs ran amok in a spree of slaughter that eventually left over 30,000 dead.

Above: The St Bartholomew's Day Massacre of 1572 left Protestant Europe profoundly in shock. Thereafter, though, it hardened attitudes. In Britain, Catholicism was soon being viewed with the deepest distrust and a visceral hostility: Protestantism and patriotism went together, it was assumed.

religion in his state; if he was Protestant, then so were his countrymen and -women. In 1618, however, that fragile peace broke down, and the first battles of the Thirty Years War were fought.

A real meat-grinder of a conflict at the heart of Europe, the Thirty Years War was fought by brutally unaccountable mercenary armies who, having no local loyalties, showed no mercy. When the Protestant city of Magdeburg was taken in 1632, for example, the population was put to the sword, some 25,000 people – mostly civilians – slaughtered. More than a fifth of

Germany's population was killed – either massacred by enemy armies or caught up in the famines and epidemics that followed the military campaign. The question of 'Who started it?' is moot, the direct responsibility of the Catholic and Protestant churches

UNHOLY COMMUNION?

WAS DESCARTES PUT to death by a priestly assassin? That suggestion has been made by one biographer, Theodor Ebert. The philosopher died in Stockholm in 1650, where he was tutor to Queen Christina; the cause of death was believed to be pneumonia. But Ebert disputes this. Sweden's Queen is known to have had a restlessly inquiring mind and to have had reservations about her country's Lutheranism: she seems to have been drawn at one time or another towards both Catholicism and freethinking. By 1649, though, she was taking active steps towards conversion to Catholicism. Concern grew that Descartes' influence might be a brake. Hence the alleged intervention of the French missionary Jacques Viogué who, says Ebert, gave the sage a communion wafer poisoned with arsenic.

in what was essentially a war between rulers debatable. Yet the episode's claim to a place in Catholicism's 'dark history' is not only indisputable but twofold: Catholics played parts as both the villains and the victims here.

Enlightened Values

Europe's religious wars had of course been deeply destructive, ugly and unedifying, but they'd at least acknowledged the centrality of faith. A disgrace to Christian ideals they may have been, but they had been fought on the assumption that their causes were worth dying for – even if they'd involved an immense amount of killing too. The Catholic view of Protestantism as diabolical heresy at least paid it the compliment of not dismissing it as a mere irrelevance. Likewise, Protestant hatred of the Church of Rome as the Painted Whore of Babylon might

be seen as preferable to a jaded dismissal as worn-out superstition, neither here nor there.

Unimaginable at the seventeenth century's start, such judgements would still have seemed recklessly outrageous at its end. But the times were definitely changing, even so. Two great thinkers had set in train a revolution in thought: René Descartes with his formula *Cogito, ergo sum* ('I think, therefore I am') in 1637, and the Englishman Isaac Newton with his *Philosophiae Materialis Principia Mathematica* ('Mathematical Principles of Natural Philosophy', 1687).

Descartes transformed the very terms of enquiry by making the human individual the first arbiter of experience. ('*I* think, therefore I am': I am my own existential guarantee.) Newton took things further: for the first time, it was possible to imagine a universe in which God's role had been drastically downscaled. This still left the problem of the 'first cause' (how could all this exist if someone hadn't made it?), but there was no necessity (perhaps no place) for a deity who, in St Matthew's formulation, 'knows every time a sparrow falls'.

Right: One of the great thinkers of the Enlightenment, the French philosopher René Descartes (1596–1650) is seen as having introduced philosophical reason to the realm of scientific enquiry and completely re-ordered our sense of what and who we are.

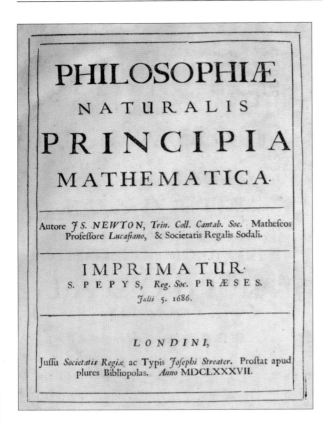

Above: Sir Isaac Newton's conception of the cosmos owed much more to scientific reason than it did to God. Whilst it didn't dispense with the idea of a creator altogether, it left 'him' badly marginalized. Newton himself believed in God – but not the divinity of Christ.

The Fighting Philosophes

It took time for these developments to filter through into the everyday thought of even the highly educated, but by the eighteenth century attitudes were changing fast. In France particularly, where the Church had associated itself closely with a corrupt and ineffectual monarchy, Catholicism was increasingly being regarded with disdain. Sophisticates were starting to embrace a new and satisfyingly scientific-sounding creed called 'deism': this accepted a creator as first cause, but went no further. God, having made the cosmos, it was suggested, had then pretty much left it to its own devices. The deity didn't concern himself with the lives of mortal men and women: 'Do you think,' asks a character in Voltaire's satirical novel *Candide* (1759) 'that when the Sultan sends a ship to Egypt he worries about whether the rats in the hold are comfortable?'

Nor, by the same token, did the supreme being care whether he was worshipped, prayed to or honoured with any of the other mumbo-jumbo offered by the Church. Which meant, in turn, that those things offered to the Church were done so under false pretences: religion was a racket, preying on the fears of the poor and superstitious. 'Theological religion', wrote Voltaire in his *Philosophical Dictionary* (1764), 'is source of all imaginable follies and disturbances; it is the parent

---

> Sophisticates were starting to embrace a new creed called 'deism': this accepted a creator as first cause, but went no further.

---

of fanaticism and civil discord. It is the enemy of mankind.' 'I have only ever uttered one prayer to God,' he said to a friend in 1767, 'and that was a very short one: "O Lord, make my enemies ridiculous." And he granted this.'

Voltaire, or to give him his real name, François-Marie Arouet (1694–1778), was one of a new breed of French writer-thinkers, the *philosophes*. Others included the scholar-journalist Denis Diderot (1713–84). The great project of his life was a vast (and, it was hoped, ultimately universal) *Encyclopedia* that would bring together all human knowledge, ascertained and organized by scientific and philosophical principles. As challenging in his own way was Diderot's friend, the Swiss-born thinker Jean-Jacques Rousseau (1712–78), with his insistence on the corrupting influence of social institutions: 'Man was born free,' he said, 'but is everywhere in chains.'

For this young generation, the Catholic Church was the enemy of truth; the spiritual arm of a reactionary order that mired the French people in benighted ignorance, abject poverty and blind superstition. It was up to modernity to clear away the obstacles to progress, to sweep away the old institutions: *Écrasez l'infâme* – 'obliterate the infamy', said Voltaire.

Opposite: With his scorching wit and his writerly esprit, François-Marie Arouet (or 'Voltaire') helped set the tone for a modernity in which brilliant sceptics would dance effortlessly around ponderous prelates, showing up the folly and corruption of the Church.

IX

MISSIONS AND MASSACRES

'Go and teach all nations…' Christ's command was a sacred trust – and a charter for paternalism and oppression. Catholic missionaries braved cruel persecution to spread their Word, but with it they took imperialistic attitudes that would give the Church a problematic place in modern history.

◆

'The people dwelling in darkness have seen a great light' – MATTHEW 4: 16

Christ's apostles had spread the Gospel through Syria and Asia Minor, and westward to Rome – which, as far as the first century was concerned, was the centre of the world. There was even a tradition that St Thomas had carried the Gospels as far as India. Several centuries of consolidation followed, but by the High Middle Ages a new spirit of evangelization was stirring: missionary work appealed to the enterprising ethic of the new friars. St Francis of Assisi had taken his followers out of the monastery and on to the road as mendicant preachers; the black-robed Dominicans were highly-motivated teachers, carrying the Christian message far and wide.

Opposite: St Francis of Assisi meets Egypt's Ayyubid Sultan Malik al-Kamil in 1219 in an effort to convert him – and bring to an end the Fifth Crusade. The later Middle Ages saw renewed attempts to spread the Christian word beyond the confines of Europe to the wider world.

Their first objective had been the revival of Catholicism in a Europe sinking into apathy and worse (this was the age of the Cathar heresy in southern France). But both orders of friars had missions to the Pagan peoples of Western and Central Asia from the thirteenth century. In 1289, Pope Nicholas IV dispatched John of Montecorvino with a party of Franciscans to take messages to Kublai Khan of China and other leading Mongols in the East. Setting up in Beijing, he built his own impressive church in which he baptized some 6000 people over 11 years, he reported proudly.

A Wider World

An impressive score, indeed – but at approximately 0.01 per cent of China's population it was clear the Middle Kingdom wasn't going to become Christian any time soon. All these early missions were necessarily small-scale ventures: geographically and politically, Christianity was confined to Europe by the forces of Islam to the east, by the Sahara to the south and by the Atlantic to the west. But the voyages of discovery

Opposite: St Francis Xavier (1506–52) was a protégé of Ignatius Loyola and founder with him of the Society of Jesus (the Jesuits). An indefatigable proselytizer, he took the Catholic message to India, Indonesia, Japan and finally to the very doorstep of China.

made by Portuguese and Spanish navigators – of whom Vasco da Gama and Columbus were only the most famous – opened up a door to a much vaster and more varied world. Out there, they found, were innumerable nations who, however different they might be in their 'civilization' or 'savagery', were all alike in never having heard of the Gospel Word.

The evangelizing impulse had never quite gone, but it had been lost sight of for a while in the confusion of the Middle Ages, in the conflicts over the papacy and the eruption of heresy in the heart of Europe. Now, however, it found a new impetus. Despite a demoralizing blow, the Church was bouncing back from the Reformation, and here were new worlds to conquer, fresh peoples to convert.

Into the East

The Jesuits led the way: in 1542, St Francis Xavier established an outpost in Goa on India's western coast. The 'Apostle of the Indies' went on to preach his faith in Indonesia and, from 1549, Japan. The other orders were not idle: the Franciscans had a mission up and running in the Sultanate of Malacca, in Malaysia, and Augustinian friars began operations in the Philippines.

China was a challenge: this vast and complex empire had its own ancient history and religious traditions. And a civilization that still, in many respects, put European culture to shame – heathens the Chinese might be, but 'benighted' never. They pushed on undaunted nonetheless. Francis Xavier was about to embark on his mission to China when he died on an

> Out there were innumerable nations who were all alike in never having heard of the Gospel Word.

island off Guangdong, on its southern coast, in 1552. Within a few decades, his fellow-Jesuits, Michele Ruggieri and Matteo Ricci, established their own mission in Beijing.

The Jesuits were welcomed by the Chinese elite and made important contacts in a scholarly and scientific community eager for fresh thinking from the West. There were few takers for Catholicism, though, and progress was hampered even further by ill-tempered competition between Jesuits and Franciscans. In 1644, in any case, Manchu invaders swept away the old regime in China, inaugurating a new order that was far less accepting of 'foreign' faiths.

CARVING UP THE EARTH

THE RIGHT OF Europe's great Catholic seagoing powers to colonize the world was never questioned: it was indeed felt that they had a duty to take the light of Christianity to those who dwelt in darkness. That the enterprise was likely to be fabulously profitable was incidental; if people were to be killed, subjugated and enslaved, the Christianizing cause was just.

The Church's greatest concern was that the new colonialism might lead to conflict at home in Europe. Separate spheres of influence for the greatest powers were going to be needed. So it was that, in Spain in 1494, in the immediate aftermath of Columbus' first

voyage and under the supervision of Pope Alexander I, the Treaty of Tordesillas was signed. This gave Portugal authority over newly-discovered territories to the east of a line (roughly) corresponding with that of longitude 48° W. Areas to the west of this line would belong to Spain.

Hence the allocation of so much of Latin America to the Spanish, along with the Philippines, while the coastal colonies of Brazil were granted to the Portuguese. In addition, Portugal could claim proprietorship over Africa and the East Indies, as well – if they could get a foothold – over China and Japan.

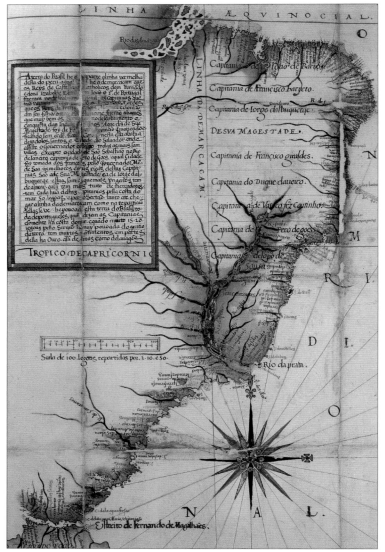

Left: The Treaty of Tordesillas (1494) had given Portugal all territories to the east of longitude 48°W. Spain got most of the New World, then – except for the eastward jutting coast of South America, now Brazil, shown here in a map of c.1579.

It wasn't until 1587 that Toyotomi Hideyoshi moved against the missionaries. The despot saw them as a threat to his centralizing rule. On Hideyoshi's orders, the foreign priests were expelled altogether from Kyushu, Japan's southwestern island, although even now individual believers were left in peace. Missionary work continued undercover and many thousands more were converted before Hideyoshi decided to seriously crack down.

In 1597, Hideyoshi decided that enough was enough. An example would have to be made if the foreigners and their culture were not to take over. On 5 February, no fewer than 26 Catholics – both foreign missionaries and Japanese converts – were publicly put to death at a mass-execution in the town of Nagasaki. Since they set so much store by Jesus' death on the cross, Hideyoshi had apparently reasoned, it was only fitting that they should themselves be crucified. A cold and sadistic logic, which might have made sense had the sufferers not gone to their deaths with a dignity that made the symbolism of the occasion irresistible. 'I have committed no crime,' said St Paul Miki – a Japanese convert to Catholicism, 'and the only reason why I am put to death is that I have been teaching the doctrine of Our Lord Jesus Christ. I am very happy to die for such a cause, and see my death as a great blessing from the Lord. At this critical time, when, you can rest assured that I will not try to deceive you, I want to stress and make it unmistakably clear that man can find no way to salvation other than the Christian way.'

Christianity was not formally abolished until 1614, but the crucifixions continued regardless. Nagasaki, the main port for European traders, was naturally the focus for missionary activity: inevitably, then, it was the

The Way of the Cross

Despite its later isolationism, Japan was welcoming to its first European visitors, survivors of a Portuguese ship that was blown onto rocks on the coast and wrecked in 1543. Even when the first missionaries arrived a few years later, relations remained cordial: the priests (from the Dominican, Franciscan and Jesuit orders) were greeted as guests of honour at the imperial court. Far from being impeded, their evangelizing activities in the decades that followed seem to have been accepted: anything up to 200,000 embraced the creed of Christ.

GOOD FOR GOA?

'I WANT TO FREE the poor Hindus from the stranglehold of the Brahmins and destroy the places where evil spirits are worshipped.' St Francis Xavier's words on arriving in Goa (1542) sound sympathetic. Except that – arguably – his priests were replacing one 'stranglehold' with another, still more constricting, as the Indians living here had already found. The Portuguese fleet had arrived here three decades before had begun by killing an estimated 10,000 Muslim defenders of what had for several centuries been an Arab Sultanate, before going on to extirpate 'Pagan' worship in the city and surrounding area. And, however pious his intentions, his proselytizing mission cannot sensibly be separated from a military campaign and administrative takeover on the part of the Portuguese which was, to all intents and purposes, imperialistic.

And so it was to continue, as can be seen from a 1566 decree by António de Noronha, the Portuguese viceroy in the region:

'I hereby order that in any area owned by my master, the king, nobody should construct a Hindu temple and such temples already constructed should not be repaired without my permission. If this order is transgressed, such temples shall be destroyed and the goods in them shall be used to meet expenses of holy deeds, as punishment of such transgression.'

The oppression only intensified into the 1580s, as an Italian visitor, the Florentine Filippo Sassetti, was to observe:

'The fathers of the Church forbade the Hindus under terrible penalties the use of their own sacred books, and prevented them from all exercise of their religion. They destroyed their temples, and so harassed and interfered with the people that they abandoned the city in large numbers, refusing to remain any longer in a place where they had no liberty, and were liable to imprisonment, torture and death if they worshipped after their own fashion the gods of their fathers.'

In the decades that followed, many thousands were to be brought before the Goa Inquisition, and untold numbers were tortured and killed. The tribunal wasn't wound up till 1812. 'Poor Hindus' indeed.

Below: St Francis Xavier's remains are kept in Goa, his first landfall in Asia, where they are housed in a great basilica built in his honour. They are brought out briefly for exposition once every ten years. Pilgrims flock to his shrine from all around the world.

focus for the crackdown too. Richard Cocks, an English sea captain, reported seeing 16 martyred in the city, 'whereof five were burned and the rest beheaded and cut in pieces, and cast into the Sea in Sackes of thirtie fathome deepe: yet the Priests got them up againe, and kept them secretly for Reliques.' Cocks noted the burning down of churches across Japan, the digging up of their hallowed graveyards and the building of pagodas and Buddhist temples in their place. All, he wrote, 'utterly to roote out the memory of Christianitie out of Japan.' At Miyako, he saw 55 Christians put to death at once, 'and among them little children five or six years old burned in their mother's arms, crying out: "Jesus receive our souls". Many more are in prison who look hourly when they shall die, for very few turn pagans.'

Japan's Catholics – native converts and European missionaries – got the message. The former decided to lay low while the latter left. When, a few years later, an attempt was made to smuggle some missionaries back in from the Philippines, it was the signal for a new wave of repression. In total 55 Christians (including the returning missionaries) were executed – burned or beheaded – and in the weeks that followed many more were martyred – whole families, including small children, condemned to a cruel death. Further pendulum-swings were to follow, as successive Shoguns either clamped down on Christianity or decided to tolerate it (partly for the sake of external trade). According to the eighteenth-century legal scholar Arai Hakuseki, another wave of persecution in the 1650s saw anything up to 300,000 converts forced to 'lean on their own staffs' – in other words, commit *hara kiri*.

Below: A fitting end for those who followed the foreign creed with all its talk of sacrifice and of walking the 'Way of the Cross'? The first of a number of mass-crucifixions in Japan was held in February 1597, at Nagasaki.

Hispaniola's Holocaust

The victims in Japan, the Catholic missionaries were very much the villain in the Americas, where conversion and subjection went hand in hand. Justified by their Christianizing mission, the Spanish conquerors pursued policies of hideous cruelty, killing and terrifying indigenous populations into submission. As Fray Bartolomé de las Casas observed at firsthand during the conquest of Hispaniola in the early sixteenth century, Christ's emissaries didn't display much in the way of love:

'They forced their way into native settlements, slaughtering everyone they found there, including small children, old men, pregnant women, and even women who had just given birth. They hacked them to pieces, slicing open their bellies with their swords as though they were sheep herded into a pen. They even placed bets on whether they could cut a man in two – or decapitate or disembowel him – at a single stroke of the axe. They grabbed suckling babies from their mothers' breasts and swung them across nearby rocks to smash

Above: The Spanish Jesuit Charles Spinola was one of several Christians – foreign missionaries and local converts – who were burned at the stake by the Shogun's officials in 1623. The crackdowns in Japan came after years of comparative tolerance, so Christianity was well-established, with a great many adherents.

their heads in – or, laughing and joking, tossed them over their shoulders into a running river. They spared no one, setting up special wide gallows on which they could set their victims dangling, their feet just off the ground, while their bodies were burned alive …'

Lest, however, their pious purpose should be forgotten in the confusion and the carnage, they hanged them thus 'thirteen at a time, in honour of Our Blessed Saviour and the Twelve Apostles'.

Indeed, concluded Las Casas, 'they invented so many new methods of murder that it would be quite impossible to put them all down on paper.' Those who survived such treatment – men, women and children alike – were set to work in the new mines and plantations, forced to carry heavy loads (and their masters in their litters) over enormous distances. In short, said Las Casas, 'they were treated as beasts of burden and developed huge sores on their shoulders and backs as happens with animals made to carry excessive loads. And this is not to mention the floggings, beatings, thrashings, punches, curses and countless other vexations and cruelties to which they were routinely subjected and to which no chronicle could ever do justice nor any reader respond save with horror and disbelief.'

In Cuba, Las Casas described how hospitable villagers brought out offerings of bread, fish and other foods for the arriving Spanish. Some 3000 men, women and children were promptly cut down in an unprovoked spree of slaughter.

Bartolomé de las Casas was a friar himself, of course, so it's only right that his courageous witness should be recorded on the positive side of the Church's historic moral ledger. Other churchmen were to do what they could to ease the condition of the conquered in the Americas, like those Jesuit missionaries whose Paraguayan *Reducciones* in Paraguay – although originally conceived as reservations (almost concentration camps) became a safe haven for the

> ... they were treated as beasts of burden and developed huge sores on their shoulders and backs as happens with animals made to carry excessive loads.

Indians from enslavement. Or like Bishop Vasco de Quiroga in Michoacán, Mexico, who did so much to protect his indigenous flock from those who would oppress them. The problem is that Las Casas' counsel was falling on deaf ears, while such credit as is due to the memory of these other benevolent priests is so overwhelmingly outweighed by the debit on the other side.

Right: Under the protection of the crucifix, Francisco Pizarro seizes the Incan King, completing his conquest of Peru. The conquistadors were to kill, rape, plunder and enslave, but the worst of the destruction they brought was quite unwitting – the introduction of germs to which New World natives were not immune.

Mexican Massacres

Hernán Cortés, who in 1521 became the conqueror of Aztec Mexico, made much of his evangelizing zeal in his letters home. As he explained to Charles V of Spain, the Aztecs had practiced human sacrifice systematically and on an appalling scale. In one of his letters, he described to his monarch how he had himself ventured into the heart of the Pagan temple in the Aztec capital, Tenochtitlán (now Mexico City). Here, he said,

'… are the images of idols, although, as I have before said, many of them are also found on the outside; the principal ones, in which the people have greatest faith and confidence, I precipitated from their pedestals, and cast them down the steps of the temple, purifying the chapels in which they had stood, as they were all polluted with human blood, shed in the sacrifices. In the place of these I put images of Our Lady and the Saints, which excited not a little feeling in Moctezuma and the inhabitants, who at first remonstrated, declaring that if my proceedings were known throughout the country, the people would rise against me; for they believed that their idols bestowed on them all temporal good, and if they permitted them to be ill-treated, they would be angry and without their gifts, and by this means the people would be deprived of the fruits of the earth and perish with famine. I answered, through the interpreters, that they were deceived in expecting any favours from idols, the work of their own hands, formed of unclean things; and that they must learn there was but one God, the universal Lord of all, who had created the Heavens and Earth, and all things else, and had made them and us; that He was without beginning and immortal, and they were bound to adore and believe Him, and no other

Opposite: Hernán Cortés rides into battle – a monstrous sight in itself for his Aztec enemy, who had no idea such things as horses might exist. Cortés' achievement was extraordinary, but he was assisted by his enemies' bewilderment in the face of firearms, armour and other strange things.

Below: Moctezuma, held hostage by the Spaniards, begs his warriors to abandon their attack as the battle for Tenochtitlán (now Mexico City) rages. Their technological advantages apart, the outnumbered conquistadors had quickly learned the advantages of pursuing a policy of divide-and-rule.

Above: Tenochtitlán fell on 13 August 1521, after a heroic last stand by the Aztec warriors. They could not prevail against European technology – or the ruthless courage of the invaders. Soon vast areas had been absorbed into a – strictly Catholic – 'New Spain'.

creature or thing. … I said everything to them I could to divert them from their idolatries, and draw them to a knowledge of God our Lord.'

Yet it hardly seems so tendentious to complain that Cortés and his men had offered 'human sacrifices' in the name of Christ on their campaign through Mexico, fighting and killing as they went. By their own testimony, they had killed 30,000 people in the city of Cholula alone; some 200,000 may have died at Tenochitlán.

In the long run, the casualties were to be a great deal higher in Mexico itself and in the Americas at large. Factor in diseases brought to the New World (albeit unwittingly) by the European conquerors and it is believed that more than 90 per cent of the population was probably wiped out.

The Requirement

Can the Church be held responsible for colonial crimes it didn't itself commit? Perhaps not, but it benefited hugely from the slaughter. It also licensed it – and this was no mere technicality but a significant thing in an age in which Europeans did genuinely fear for the

fate of their immortal souls and might at least have tempered their excesses if encouraged to do so by their moral guides. It's been fashionable as late to scoff at the 'religious' motives of those now seen as entirely cynical, brutal opportunists – and such scepticism is fair enough, up to a point. It's nevertheless surely significant that, for what it's worth, these Spanish conquerors invariably took pains to read the *Requerimiento* ('Requirement') aloud – and have it formally witnessed by a notary – to any indigenous chief or monarch they met before his realms were ransacked and his people killed or captured. Ludicrous as it may seem now, this document did underline the 'legitimacy' of such depredations and made clear the connection between the colonialists and the Catholic Church:

'[I] hereby notify and inform you that God Our Lord, One and Eternal, created Heaven and Earth and a man and woman from whom you and I and all the

UP FOR DEBATE

In 1550–51, an important debate was held in Valladolid, then the Spanish capital. Two Dominicans, Fray Juan Ginés de Sepúlveda and Fray Bartolomé de las Casas, took the floor. Up for discussion was the question of whether the indigenous peoples of 'New Spain' should be considered human, in the way that Europeans were. On the one hand, the explorers reported, they looked like humans – at least superficially: they stood upright; had heads, arms, legs and unfurred skin as humans did. On the other, it was said, they went about their lives completely naked, just like animals, and they had none of those technologies or skills that signalled civilization to Europeans.

Were such beings to be treated as equals? Or should they be taken under subjection for their own sake? Sepúlveda eloquently argued the latter case. Had not Aristotle himself written that some peoples were by their very nature slaves, and needed to be subjected for their own good? On the contrary, Las Casas maintained, the 'Indians' were entitled to exactly the same treatment as Europeans. Although, as he went on to argue, these rights were being scandalously ignored. Las Casas' was the first influential voice to be raised against the cruelty of European colonialism and Catholic evangelism in the New World.

Below: At the Valladolid Debate, Spain's Charles I (Emperor Charles V) consulted clerical advisers. Here Fray Juan de Quevedo and Bartolomé de las Casas make the case that America's 'uncivilized' natives all are human – and all equally worthy of respect.

peoples of the world are descended ... God placed one man named St Peter in charge of all these peoples ... So it is that I request and require you to acknowledge the Church as your mistress and as Governess of the World and the Universe, and the High Priest or Pope in Her name and His Majesty in his place, as Ruler, Lord and King.'

If the hearer didn't heed this 'request', the document continued:

'I will come against you in overwhelming force, and make war on you in every way I can and subject you to the yoke and the obedience of the Church and of His Majesty the King, and I will take your women and children and make them slaves ... The responsibility for the death and destruction this will bring will rest with you.'

Risorgimento and Retreat

Throughout the Age of Discovery and on through the Enlightenment era, the geographical reach of the Church was being steadily extended in the New World. Ironically, though, the conditions were already being created – in the philosophical and scientific scepticism of Descartes and his successors – for the erosion of its importance at home in Europe.

Even in 'Catholic' countries the Church was in retreat. Nationalism was on the rise among an increasingly affluent and educated urban middle class that wanted autonomy and freedom for the individual as well as for country. Marx might have dismissed the resulting turbulence as a 'bourgeois revolution' but it was quite corrosive enough as far as Catholicism was concerned. Italy itself wasn't to be spared: the

Below: Catholic America (sporting the simian features of Thomas Nast's cartoon-Irish) seeks to assist an unceremoniously unseated Pope Pius IX. Dislodged from the Papal States by a moustachioed Victor Emmanuel, King of the New Italy, the Pope was most indignant, but most Americans beheld his plight unmoved.

Opposite: Pius IX appears with more dignity in this respectful portrait. More dignity than he actually possessed, it might be argued. In an apparent headlong flight from modernity, Pius took a succession of what now seem desperate measures to shore up the failing authority of the Church.

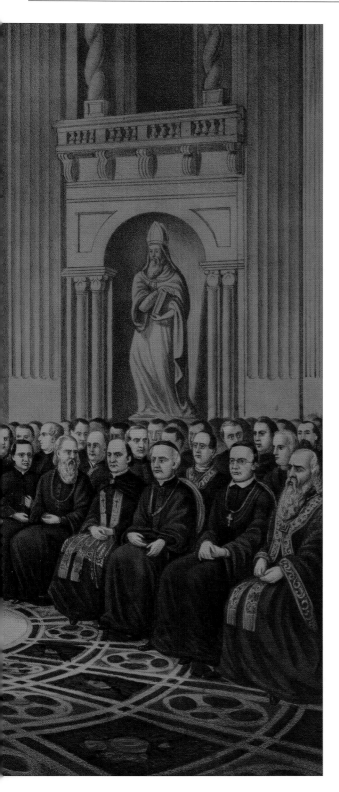

Risorgimento or 'Resurgence' which swept the country in the nineteenth century was not such good news for the Vatican. The new mood of cultural self-esteem and the political confidence this brought with it made it apparent that the new Italy was in no mood to take any orders from the Church. The papacy was squeezed

---

Alarmingly, Pius IX's 'Syllabus of Errors' – an index of ills in the modern world – included free speech and religious toleration.

– quite literally, it might be said, the Papal States first forced to democratize, then absorbed into a unified Italy. Confined to his own little corner of Rome, the Vatican Palace still nominally (if a little incongruously) a sovereign state, the Pope cut an increasingly beleaguered figure.

As of 1870, indeed, Pius IX was the self-proclaimed 'Prisoner of the Vatican', although the only obstacle to his leaving was his own papal pride. The Church has never been conspicuously forward-looking, perhaps, but its longstanding resistance to radical change and its profound suspicion of liberalism and all its works were undeniably underscored by the humiliations of this time. The assumption that there was a natural affinity between Catholicism and what might loosely be called the 'forces of reaction' was to dog the Church for a century and more.

Pius' passive-aggressive self-imprisonment only underlined an intellectual retreat he'd been making since the 1860s when he'd started drawing up his 'Syllabus of Errors' – an increasingly baggy, catch-all index of all the Vatican thought was wrong with the modern world. Alarmingly, it included things such as free speech and religious toleration. It was of course Pope Pius IX who, in 1869, staged the First Vatican Council – the convention that definitively recorded the dogma of papal infallibility. Could it have been a coincidence that the first Pope ever to feel the need to

Left: Pius IX presides over the First Vatican Council (1869) with quiet authority – if only his writ had run beyond the palaces of Rome. Increasingly beleaguered, Pius set his Church against modernity, storing up problems which have even now to be resolved.

ABDUCTED BY THE POPE

EDGARDO MORTARA ALMOST met his maker when he was a few weeks old in 1851, when he was very nearly carried off by a bout of fever. So badly had his condition scared the servant girl looking after him that at one point she'd splashed him with water in an emergency baptism. An understandable reaction in a devoutly Catholic young woman, perhaps – no matter that Edgardo and his family were Jewish. Edgardo got better and the whole thing was forgotten until a few years later when he was seven and the affair was brought to light. Edgardo had been raised in the Jewish faith – but this was against the law in what were still the Papal States, where canon law prevailed over all else. The authorities felt they had no alternative but to take Edgardo away from his outraged parents: it was forbidden for any Catholic child to be brought up in a non-Catholic home. So it was that young Edgardo grew up the adoptive child of the Holy Father: a vociferous campaign by his desolate parents and by Jewish and liberal activists couldn't shake Pope Pius IX's resolve to keep him. Or, in fairness, Edgardo's to stay: reaching adulthood in 1870 when the Papal States ceased to be, he made his own choice to continue in the Church and become a priest.

always be right had this set down as dogma at a time when his true authority was coming under question?

In a sense, successive Popes were going to be 'Prisoners of the Vatican' for a while: Pius' withdrawal from the world marked the start of a 70-year sulk.

Into Africa

The Church's precarious position in a changing Europe meant it had all the more reason for looking outward. In the colonialist 'Scramble for Africa' it was well to the fore – but in a background role, of course. While the great European powers aggrandized themselves, the Church helped out with behind-the-scenes support, the spiritual arm of imperialist expansion in Africa. (Not that the Catholic Church was alone by any means. From the start of the 'Scramble' in the 1880s, the sun never set on the work of Anglican and Protestant missionaries spreading the Word of British supremacy along with that of God.)

Railways and the rule of law went hand in hand with enslavement and exploitation; savage repression in pursuit of a 'civilizing' mission. The legacy of colonialism in a 'Dark Continent' apparently all the gloomier for European intervention has been hotly debated down the decades since.

The same sort of weighing of one thing against another has to take place for the Church's contribution to be assessed. Missionary priests and nuns may have fed the starving, nursed the sick and educated children – weren't they just 'enabling' oppression, though, overall?

Sometimes they went much further. Even in the annals of colonialism, the story of the Congo Free State (CFS) stands out in its acts of cruelty: between 1885 and 1908 over ten million people are believed to have died. At this time what was later to be the 'Belgian Congo' (and later still the Democratic Republic of Congo) was pretty much a private enterprise, bought and owned personally by Belgium's King Leopold II. The grotesqueness of the project started with its scale (the CFS covered well over 70 times the area of Belgium itself) but went on to include an administrative system bordering on insanity. Massacres were almost routine – whole communities killed to 'encourage the others' to work harder. Rape was not just a soldiers' 'perk' but a means of social discipline. No taboo was sacred when it came to instilling the fear of God and Leopold's Congo Company: boys were forced to have sex with their sisters – their mothers, even. Production norms, in agriculture, rubber-tapping or mining, were enforced by physical mutilation: if you didn't meet your target, you lost your hand.

Opposite: Belgium's Leopold II, a giant constricting snake, crushes the Congo in his 'rubber coils'. (Rubber was among the most lucrative crops being cultivated there.) Though not directly responsible for perhaps the cruellest colonization of modern times, the Church played an important ancillary role.

Above: Forced labourers carry equipment in the Congo for their colonial overlords. The prevailing view in Europe, and in a Church which was European in its attitudes, was that Africa was a 'Dark Continent' that should be converted – by force if necessary – and set to work.

The Church's culpability in one of modern colonialism's most terrible atrocities is disputed. And with some reason. Individual priests spoke out against the abuses at the time. Officially, moreover, the Church took no part in and had no influence over what was primarily a matter of policy in the power of Leopold and his managers in what amounted to a commercial company. But the Church's notorious child-colonies

didn't just take in orphans: in the long term they created more. These institutions fed directly into the *Force Publique* – the notorious paramilitary police force of the Free State, the vicious instrument of official terror in the country. Parentless boys were brought up by the missionaries to identify entirely with the occupying authorities and see their own people as an enemy to be raped, mutilated, killed and generally kept down.

The cruelty didn't come from one side only: Catholic converts were among the 45 or so young Christians burned alive at Namagongo (in modern Uganda) in 1886. As pageboys of the King of Buganda, Mwanga II, they might have expected to be protected by their status, but their lord had started to feel threatened by the inroads the foreign missionaries were making among his people. Rulers like Mwanga were right to feel that their position was precarious, and that Christianity was (as it were) oiling the wheels of a European takeover in East Africa.

Opposite: Twenty-two Ugandan Catholics (as well as a number of Anglican converts) were killed by King Mwanga II in the 1880s. This banner commemorates their canonization, which took place in 1964 as the Church woke up to the importance of its role in Africa.

WHITE FATHERS, WHITE RULE

THEY WERE WHITE themselves, of course, but it was their dress that gained the Society of Missionaries of Africa their common nickname as the *Pères Blancs* or 'White Fathers' from their foundation by Charles Lavigerie.

Their robes – pure white from head to foot – offered a sort of homage to those of the Arabs of the Sahara region, where their missions got under way in

the 1870s. They subsequently pushed south and east, doing genuinely heroic service (several were killed by hostile tribesmen) in what are now Mali, Sudan, the Central African Republic, Uganda and Burundi.

Although their work was peaceful in itself, its strategic value should not be ignored. The Presence of Cardinal Lavigerie in Tunis, remarked one French statesman, 'is worth an army to France'.

THE DEVIL'S CENTURY

Wars, revolutions, genocides, terror campaigns, coups and assassinations: the twentieth century saw one enormity after another. The Catholic Church was variously a victim of and a witness to – in some cases arguably an accessory in – some of the greatest crimes of modern times.

◆

'When the thousand years are ended, Satan will be released from his prison.' – REVELATION 20: 7

Herzegovina, 1981. A country under Communism; a state swallowed up, indeed, in the Socialist Federal Republic of Yugoslavia. A valiant fighter against Nazi oppression, Marshal Tito had been accorded a certain respect, however grudging, by the people he had ruled over through the post-War years. But Josip Broz – to give him his birth-name – had finally died the year before; his successors had seemed less worthy of their status. For the moment, though, their power remained in place: not until the early 1990s would civil war start to sweep Yugoslavia and the country fall apart in acrimony and bloodshed.

Opposite: For the Catholic Church – as for the world – the twentieth century seemed a catalogue of tragedy. Marshal Tito's funeral in Belgrade in 1980 marked the end of a time of tyranny – but brought a new one of genocidal violence.

Nestling in the mountains not far from the Croatian border, Medjugorje was a beautiful and peaceful place – deceptively so, for the scene of a notorious massacre four decades before. In 1941, during the Second World War, over a thousand Serbs had been slaughtered by Croats from the fascistic *Ustase* movement and thrown into mass-graves which then remained unmarked – and yet not unremembered by a people still in pain.

Small wonder, then, that when the Virgin Mary appeared to a group of children here they should have paid particularly close attention to her view of recent history. This, the twentieth century, had, she told them, been the century over which Satan had presided. God had agreed to let him take a turn in charge of the universe as a test for his Church down here on Earth. Hence, from a parochial point of view, the sufferings of a Yugoslavia whose twentieth century had already been all but unbearable – even if in the years to come it was going to get a great deal worse. And hence a global history in which tyrannies of Right and Left had vied in cruelty, terror and violence had almost become the norm.

It should be stressed from the start that the Medjugorje visions have been controversial, even within Catholicism; senior churchmen have expressed grave doubts about the seers' testimony. What cannot seriously be disputed is that the twentieth century was to prove a particularly trying time for the Roman Catholic Church – as it was, indeed, for humanity as a whole.

Mexican Mayhem

'For the ten years from 1910 to 1920,' historian Thomas Benjamin has written, 'Mexicans devoted most of their energy to war and destruction.' A damning summary, yet one with which it's difficult to disagree. So violence against the Catholic clergy (and counter-violence committed in the Church's name) have both to be seen in the context of this wider conflagration. The Mexican Revolution was an almost unbelievably bloody and anarchic affair, its violence only very vaguely directed towards a final goal.

As elsewhere in a Hispanic world in which the Church was clearly identified with conservative landowning interests, anticlericalism and political radicalism went hand in hand. The two great rebel leaders, Pancho Villa and Emiliano Zapata, were very different characters, with widely divergent views, but neither had any time for the Catholic Church. Neither did the urban intelligentsia – many of them freemasons – whose self-conscious progressiveness made them contemptuous of a Catholicism that many workers and peasants resented as being parasitical on the poor. Attacks on priests and churches were frequent during the fighting – when the city of Durango was sacked by Pancho Villa's men in 1913, the embroidered mantle from the Blessed Virgin in the cathedral ended up adorning the shoulders of a bandit's mistress. Convents were attacked and nuns were raped; churches were plundered and burned and images desecrated.

When some sort of constitutional rule was restored in 1917, anti-Catholic feeling – far from coming to an end – was institutionalized. The 'Calles Law', while nominally just ensuring the scrupulous separation of Church and State, went a great deal further in

Left: Rumours of the 'Death of God' in the twentieth century turned out to have been exaggerated. People turned out in their joyful thousands in 2001 to celebrate the twentieth anniversary of the first vision of the Virgin Mary at Medjugorje, in Bosnia.

circumscribing the rights of the Catholic clergy. (Church property was confiscated; Catholic schools were shut down and convents closed. Even wearing a priestly cassock in public was outlawed.) It also arguably gave tacit 'permission' for cruder and more violent discrimination at grass-roots level. Certainly, that was the message that filtered down to rabble-rousers in city neighbourhoods and small towns. It isn't known how many priests were murdered: only a few dozen were openly lynched, while many hundreds fled the country. By the mid-1920s, though, between official restrictions and popular harassment, in large

parts of Mexico there were none left. An attempt by Catholic *Cristeros* to fight back from 1927 was met with savage violence: 90,000 were to die on both sides during this three-year civil war.

Opium and Opprobrium

In Russia, too, anticlericalism was the default position among a revolutionary caste ever mindful of Marx's view that religion was 'the opium of the people'. Through most of the Soviet republics summoned into existence by the Revolution of 1917, Christianity was represented by the Orthodox Church, but the implications for Catholicism were to be profound in the longer term.

For the first few years at least, the Soviet achievement was an inspiration for downtrodden workers in the West who saw in it the opportunity

Below: Basking in their new-found power, Zapata and his men prepare for government – and the liberation of a landlord-ridden, priest-infested country. For many in Mexico the Church was no more than the spiritual arm of the ruling class; an enemy which had to be destroyed.

Above: Ransacked by Russian Bolsheviks, this tattered, messy and rubble-strewn scene is emblematic of the situation of the Catholic Church in the Soviet sphere. Allowed to eke out an ignominious existence, it could never feel any real autonomy – nor ever, really, that it was in any sense secure.

for real change; and, by the same token, they saw the Church of Rome as instinctively reactionary, a brake on progress towards a better, fairer world. Nor did the Catholic hierarchy disappoint, denouncing all attempts at social or political reform as godless Communism and driving thoughtful men and women into the intellectual embrace of the Bolsheviks.

Flirting with Fascism

For many, in Italy and in the world outside, the Lateran Treaty dragged the Church still deeper into disrepute.

Signed in 1929, it granted the Church its own little sovereign state in the Vatican City while at the same time guaranteeing its political neutrality and accepting the constitutional arrangements prevailing across Italy as a whole. As far as it went this was no great betrayal, perhaps – successive Italian governments had been pressing for something similar; and later administrations have honoured the Treaty to this day. What upset progressive Catholics was the fact that Pope Pius XI had reached this accommodation with Mussolini, the Great Dictator, and was effectively pledging the Church's allegiance to his Fascist state.

In return, Mussolini won concessions: massive compensation for the loss of the old Papal States (over which the Church had been moping and moaning since 1871, when Pius IX had made himself the prisoner of the Vatican). *Il Duce* – despite his own personal

Above: Not quite a pact with the devil, perhaps, but the next best thing in the Italy of the 1920s, Pope Pius XI signs his Concordat with Mussolini. In its obsessive concern with resisting Communism, the Church was to overlook all sorts of offences in its allies.

Opposite: A cathedral goes up in flames at the climax of Spain's 'Red Terror' of 1936. The Left's suspicions of the Church, as the reactionaries' first line of defence, were by no means entirely unfounded, though they were certainly to some degree self-fulfilling.

scorn – appointed Catholicism the state religion, made criticism of the Church a crime, outlawed divorce and made religious education mandatory in the country's schools. All state legislation was to be reviewed to ensure that it stayed in line with canon law. No one imagined for a moment that Mussolini had undergone a Damascene conversion of any kind. He made no secret of his continuing disdain. But Fascism (till now dismissed as an ideology of thugs) had secured the respectability it had craved, whilst Pius XI declared Mussolini 'a man sent by providence'.

The Cross and the Carnage

In Spain, it seemed that providence favoured the overthrow of the elected government and its replacement by a murderous military dictatorship.

So, at least, it must be concluded from the Church's unstinting support for Francisco Franco and his friends. Not that this was such a surprise. Those leaders of the Spanish armed forces who staged an uprising against the elected Republican government in 1936 did so, they said, in defence of traditional Spanish values – among which Catholicism was key. On the Left, this was quite clearly understood: in the summer of 1936 it was the clergy who bore the brunt of the 'Red Terror'. Churches were burned and convents ransacked, and in a matter of weeks some 60,000 people (including 6800 priests) were killed.

Inevitably, perhaps, the Red Terror was followed by a 'White' one, as Franco's forces exacted their cruel tit-for-tat. Not that they'd needed any such excuse: hatred of the Left was deeply embedded in the

A CARNIVAL OF BLASPHEMY

MUCH LESS SERIOUS than the slaughter of Spanish priests in real terms, but in its way every bit as significant at a symbolic level, was what Archbishop Antonio Montero Moreno has since referred to as the 'martyrdom of objects'. The bodies of priests and nuns were dragged up from crypts, their open coffins piled up in city streets; statues of saints were smashed, disfigured or put together as if to copulate; churches were turned into dance halls and storage depots; religious vestments were seized and mock-processions held through jeering, spitting crowds. Class and religious resentments went together: typically, affluent conservatives identified with the Church. Rounded up by anarchist gangs, bourgeois believers were forced to utter blasphemies before they were shot, their executioners enjoying the thought that these well-heeled holy joes and josephines wouldn't be dying in a state of grace.

officer-class, who wore their crucifixes and rosaries as a badge of honour, and who saw the Church as not only the emblem but the spiritual justification for the society they saw themselves as building. 'We shall,' said General Emilio Mola, 'build a great, strong, powerful state that is set to be crowned with a cross.' Where other right-wing dictators of the era attempted

> Suffice it to say though that the Catholic Church – not just in Spain itself, but beyond in Rome – was to be an important cheerleader for General Franco.

to absorb religious institutions into those of an all-encompassing (hence 'totalitarian') state, the *Caudillo* saw the Church as sacred, his administration as its protector. In Spain, in recent years, debate has been raging over whether Franco can truly be characterized as having been a 'Fascist'.

And his conservative cheerleaders are right: technically he wasn't – for what the distinction's worth. The Catholic Church cannot of course be held wholly

Opposite: Christ and Caesar were too cosy by half in the Spain of General Franco. Here the *Caudillo* visits Cardinal Federico Tedeschini, the Papal Nuncio. Franco's regime murdered men, women and children in their tens of thousands with the Church's tacit blessing. The whereabouts of over 114,000 victims are still unknown.

responsible for the 'White Terror' and the 200,000-odd deaths it's believed to have brought; neither can the extent of its culpability be easily quantified. Suffice it to say though that the Catholic Church – not just in Spain itself, but beyond in Rome – was to be an important cheerleader for Franco. Not just during the Civil War but in the years after when his murderous regime was otherwise to a large extent excluded from the world community.

The Holy Father and the Fatherland
Friedrich Nietzsche, notoriously, had dismissed Christianity for its 'slave morality'. Turning the other cheek assuredly wasn't Adolf Hitler's style. Like Mussolini, born a Catholic, the future *Führer* had turned his back on the Church as he grew older and began to conceive his vocation as leader of an all-conquering Aryan Fatherland.

Even for the leader of the Third Reich, though, there were realities that had to be recognized. One was the considerable number of Catholics in Germany, especially in the South. A naturally conservative constituency, they remained wary of Hitler and his National Socialists. Hence Hitler's overtures to Pope Pius XI, who hoped to secure the position of the Church in a changing Germany and find an ally in his opposition to the Communist advance in Europe.

Pius, who four years earlier had signed a similar Concordat with Mussolini, had no hesitation in agreeing to the treaty. The Concordat he signed in 1933 may have been seen by the Pope as nothing more than a diplomatic recognition of political practicalities, but Hitler was able to exhibit it as though it were a sacred blessing.

The Nazis made more uncomfortable bedfellows than the Italian Fascists had, their ugly anti-Semitism soon apparent to the world. In 1937, abashed, the

Pope went so far as to send out an encyclical – a letter to be read in German churches – entitled *Mit Brennender Sorge* ('With Burning Sorrow'). It contained an outspoken condemnation of the Nazis' attacks upon their country's Jews as well as their efforts to control the activities of the Catholic Church in Germany. So horrified had Pius XI become by Hitler's influence, he'd finally concluded that he was possessed by the devil and had attempted to exorcise him at long-distance.

Below: The future Pope Pius XII, Eugenio Pacelli, was Papal Nuncio in Germany. Here he leaves the Presidential Palace in Berlin. That Pacelli 'went native' with the Nazis is untrue – he disdained their brutish views – yet he never seems to have appreciated the enormity of their crimes.

JEWISH QUESTIONS

THE CHURCH'S REPUTATION is for dogmatic certainty (even where such certainty may be ill-advised) but it can be as woolly and ambivalent as any other institution. So it was with its wartime conduct – a dereliction of duty never really redeemed by isolated acts of humanity and courage; so it was in its pre-war attitudes to the Jews. Blanket charges of 'anti-Semitism' against the Church are easily enough refuted by specific examples – but then so too are blanket exonerations. While the medieval idea that the Jews should be collectively condemned as the 'killers of Christ' was now no longer being preached, many in the Vatican still saw 'the Jews' as a deadly threat. In 1929, one spokesman, Father Enrico Rosa, drew what he clearly saw as a scrupulous distinction between an unworthy and un-Christian racial anti-Semitism and a 'healthy evaluation of the danger emanating from the Jews'. His fellow-Jesuit Gustav Gundlach teased out his argument a little further the following year. To hate the Jews *because* they were Jews – and, as such, intrinsically alien and 'other' – was deplorable, he argued. To hate them because they were cosmopolitan in their loyalties and damaging in their influence in the arts, the media, science and finance was quite another thing. The 'Chosen People' of Old Testament times, it seems, were now the vanguard of all that was dangerously modern; the enemies of established Western values.

'Hitler's Pope'?

The 1933 Concordat had been negotiated by a young and energetic cardinal, Eugenio Pacelli – a lover of Germany and its culture, and a conservative through and through. As Pope Pius XII from 1939, he was to steer the Church through the stormy waters of the Second World War – wrecking its moral reputation, many have suggested, in the process. Pius' characterization – caricaturing, even – as 'Hitler's Pope', is arguably harsh: relations between the two men were seldom cordial and never easy. There is little doubt, though, that Pius saw in Hitler just what the German *Führer* saw in him: a man with whom – whatever his drawbacks – he could do business.

The Holocaust is rightly remembered as one of the very darkest episodes of modern history, the Church one of many institutions that fell badly short. And this is especially significant, given the moral authority it has historically claimed; the right it has assumed to tell its members – and the wider world – how it should live. Pius XII's defenders have pointed to the good he did – justifiably, up to a point: it's easily forgotten that the young Pacelli had actually been the author of the impassioned plea against racism in *Mit Brennender Sorge*. And it's been demonstrated too that, as Pope, he organized rescue measures in the Vatican City that led to the saving of a great many Jewish lives. But the good he did was invariably done by stealth. When the world looked to him for leadership he was silent – at best equivocal. An unabashed elitist, he despised National Socialism for its vulgar populism, but doesn't seem to have been as outraged by its morality as he might have been. He wasn't a Nazi; nor could he even be charged of an indifference to the threat it posed – but he was more exercised by the threat represented by Communism in the east.

What can be said of Pius goes for the Church as a whole: it isn't difficult to find ways in which good was done and evil resisted. Many individual priests and nuns performed acts of astounding courage to save Jewish families from death in Germany. And the authorities reacted, rounding up what they saw as their enemies: Dachau alone housed 2600 priests. In Poland, national resistance to the German invaders was largely coordinated by the Catholic clergy. Some 2500 priests in that country were to be executed by the Nazis. Overall, though, the fact remains that the Final Solution was a challenge dismally ducked: the Church has been struggling to reassert its moral authority ever since.

Poland Oppressed

Poland's problem, in the post-War era, wasn't to come from Nazism but from Communism. The Red Army liberated it only to take it under Soviet rule. The

Church clung on here, in an excruciatingly uneasy co-existence with a socialist government that wouldn't let it flourish openly yet never felt quite strong enough to stamp it out completely. Important leaders were arrested and imprisoned – thousands tortured. As elsewhere behind the Iron Curtain, a state-sponsored pseudo-Church was created, but the people of Poland were never fooled. Even so, Catholicism struggled to maintain a meaningful presence in the country. Pope John Paul II, born Karol Wojtyła, was many years later to talk of Poland's 'Silent Church' – capable of offering some degree of comfort and continuity, but not to raise its voice in spiritual leadership.

> One priest more than any other articulated the aspirations of Poles for freedom at this time: Jerzy Popiełuszko preached each week at his Warsaw church.

When Poland's people *did* eventually find their voice, though, it was in response to the pastoral visit of Pope John Paul II himself, who came soon after his election in 1979. They turned out to see him in their hundreds of thousands: in all, it's estimated, a third of the Polish population came to see him celebrate a series of open-air masses. The Communist authorities didn't like it but didn't dare object. That visit seems to have emboldened Poland, helping to inspire the setting-up of *Solidarnosc* (the 'Solidarity' movement) in 1980.

The Church continued to lend crucial support. After General Jaruzelski's government imposed martial law in December 1981, the workers' meetings with which the *Solidarnosc* campaign had started were forbidden – but people could still come together to celebrate mass. One priest more than any other articulated the aspirations of Poles for freedom at this time: Jerzy Popiełuszko preached each week at his Warsaw church. In 1984, its patience exhausted, the state had its agents stage a car crash for Popiełuszko's

Right: The cross has been conceived on the gigantic scale formerly reserved for Soviet war memorials and Lenin statues: Pope John Paul II's trip to Poland (1979) – the first major engagement of his pontificate – was both a joyful homecoming and a warning to the regime.

Above: Pope John Paul II makes a point to General Wojciech Jaruzelski. But Poland's Prime Minister was not convinced. Even so, throughout the 1980s, Catholicism remained an inspiration for patriotic Poles fighting to free their country from Communist oppression.

benefit. He escaped unhurt, but was seized and abducted a few days later. He was beaten to death, his body abandoned by the side of a reservoir, a martyr for Catholicism – and his country.

The Latin Masses

If the fight against Communism had brought out the best in the Catholic Church in Poland, the same could hardly be said of what had happened in South America. Since the 1970s, the Church had allied itself strongly with some of the most unpleasant regimes in the world in Augusto Pinochet's Chile and the Generals' Argentina. Like the United States establishment, the Church had viewed the region with mounting concern for many years – since Fidel Castro's Cuban Revolution of 1959, indeed.

Latin America's poor and dispossessed masses had seemed 'naturally' to be the property of the Church – a vast and unquestioningly obedient congregation. That they might now be seizing the opportunity to liberate themselves caused consternation. In the paranoia of the Cold War era, any sign of popular unrest was viewed with trepidation; any stirrings of student radicalism denounced as communistic. Even as priests in Poland risked their lives for freedom, the Church in Argentina and Chile was turning a blind eye while suspected activists were abducted, tortured and killed, their bodies dumped by roadsides or dropped from helicopters far out at sea. In Chile in 1973, the democratically elected government of the Marxist Salvador Allende had been overthrown in a bloody

Opposite: The image of Father Jerzy Popiełuszko is carried in procession through the streets of Warsaw in celebration of his beatification on 6 June 2010. Patriotism and piety have gone together in a Poland whose Catholic religion was repressed along with its people under Communism.

coup by the country's military, led by General Augusto Pinochet.

Three years later in Argentina, fearing a similar drift into disorder and Marxist revolution, the leading generals seized power. In both countries, the military set to work stamping out any sign of resistance, snatching up dissidents from their homes and from city streets. Most were never to be seen again: in Argentina alone, these *desaparecidos* ('disappeared ones') numbered getting on for 30,000. Estimates for those killed and missing in Pinochet's Chile are only slightly less.

Below: 'The disappeared cry out for Justice!' And so did their suffering mothers and other relations through the long and bitter years of Argentina's 'Dirty War'. Many priests were sympathetic – some were 'disappeared' by the Generals' thugs themselves – but the hierarchy tended to side with the right-wing regime.

Welcome as it was in many ways, the election of the Argentine Cardinal Jorge Bergoglio as Pope Francis in 2013 called attention to a time many in the Church had been trying to forget. As so often in the Church's history, a great many priests, nuns and ordinary Catholics had acquitted themselves with commitment and courage on behalf of their people: once again, though, it seemed that the hierarchy had let them down. The part played by the American CIA in supporting General Pinochet's coup in 1973 has been much publicized. Less well known is the support he received from the Catholic Church. In the days following the coup – a time in which over 3000 civilians were murdered – the Chilean Episcopal Conference asked the people to assist the government in its 'difficult task of restoring national order and the economic life of the country, so seriously affected'. In Argentina too, senior churchmen lent the military

Above: La Moneda, Santiago, was bombed by the Chilean air force in the military coup which brought General Pinochet to power in 1973. The country's elected Marxist President, Salvador Allende, who committed suicide inside his palace, had been deeply distrusted both by the United States and by the Church.

junta at least their tacit support, although many priests and nuns fought hard for freedom and justice at parish level. Unsurprisingly, the role of the future Pope Francis has been hotly contested since his appointment, although claims that he collaborated with the dictatorship, betraying his own priests, remain unsubstantiated.

Catholic Communism?

Liberation Theology may have been a bastard creed, but it inspired real heroism in many of its adherents. As first outlined by the Peruvian priest Gustavo Gutiérrez, the 'Theology of Liberation' demanded a radically-overhauled Catholicism which would work to bring about change in this world, not just happiness in the next. No longer would it be the 'opium of the people': it would be a formula for revolutionary transformation of society. Many thousands of priests, nuns and lay Catholics heard Gutiérrez's Gospel and were inspired.

Many were to die for their beliefs. In Colombia, Camilo Torres, announcing that 'if Christ were alive today, he would be a guerrilla,' enlisted with his country's Marxist National Liberation Army, in whose service he was killed during his first action in 1966. Archbishop Oscar Romero, who from his pulpit led popular opposition to El Salvador's oppressive military regime, was assassinated at the altar as he said mass one day in 1980. Clerics were also well represented among the Sandinistas who came to power in Nicaragua in the 1980s, including the priest and poet Ernesto Cardenal.

The Church was not impressed. Even when its own nuns were raped and murdered by right-wing death squads in El Salvador, it seemed more concerned about the risk of Communist contamination in the Church. Pope John Paul II's experiences of life in Poland almost certainly helped to shape his sceptical reaction to Liberation Theology, despite his own well-documented

Above: Born in Lima, in 1928, Gustavo Gutiérrez grew up to become a Dominican friar – and founder of 'Liberation Theology'. So central was Christ's command to help the poor, Gutiérrez argued, that his disciples had a duty to fight for revolution.

Opposite: Nuns seek in vain to save the life of Archbishop Oscar Romero of El Salvador. An ally of the poor, he had been gunned down by members of a right-wing death squad while saying mass.

concern for social justice. (In September 2013, Pope Francis raised eyebrows by giving the aged Gustavo Gutiérrez, by now 85, an audience. Was Liberation Theology about to get a second chance?)

Bank of Brothers

Early in the morning of 18 June 1982, the body of a man was found hanging from scaffolding underneath an arch of London's Blackfriars Bridge. Squeezed into his pockets with eight bricks for weight was $14,000 in three different currencies: this had been no ordinary suicide – if that was even what it was. The dead man was soon identified as an Italian, Roberto Calvi, chairman of the Banco Ambrosiano who had gone missing from his home in Milan some days before.

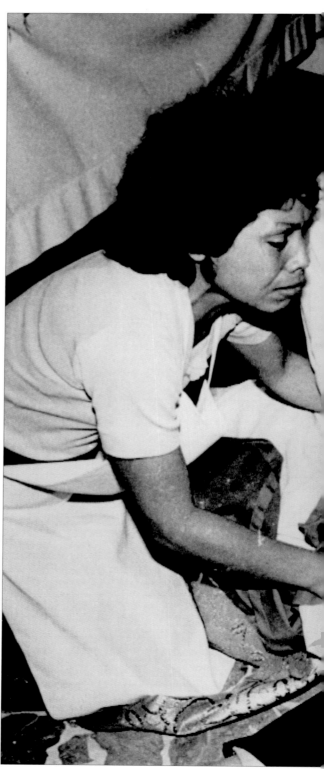

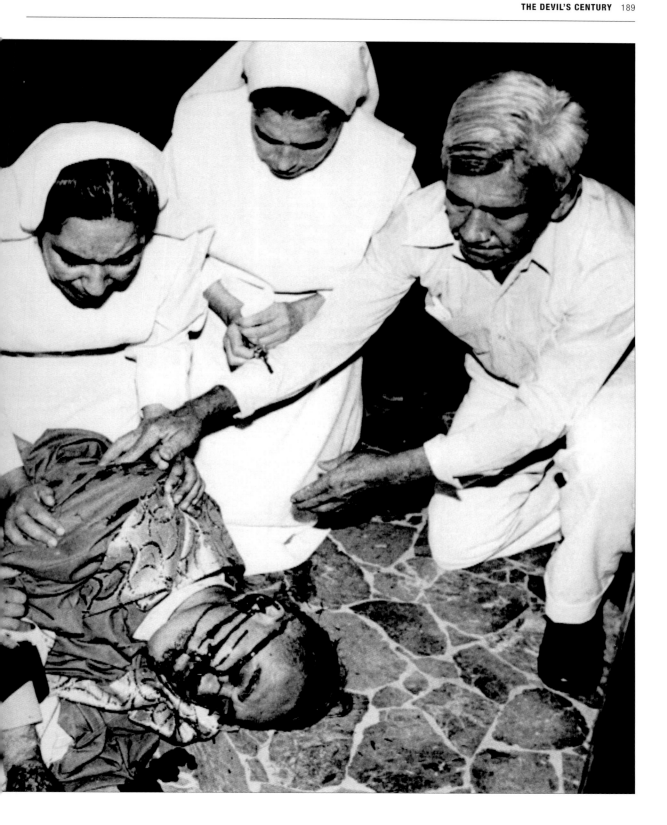

DIRTY TRICKS

THE HISTORY OF South and Central America in the second half of the twentieth century was – to put it mildly – messy and unpleasant. Discussion has tended to focus on the role of the United States, and more specifically the secret activities of the CIA in what was seen as 'America's Backyard'. In Central America particularly, the interests of US business were seen as paramount: the Free World had to be made safe for United Fruit. Yet other organizations had much at stake as well – none more than the Roman Catholic Church, which looked to Latin America as a secure heartland of belief.

When we read of US support for the monstrous regime of Rafael Trujillo, who terrorized the Dominican Republic for 30 years from 1930 to 1961, we shouldn't forget the vital support he was given by the Church. At a time when even the US was losing faith in their sometime puppet, his Concordat with the Vatican (1954) came to his rescue, giving him the one shred of diplomatic legitimacy he had. That same year, while the CIA was parachuting arms with Soviet markings into Guatemala to smear Jacobo Arbenz's reforming government, New York's Cardinal Francis Spellman was burning up the wires to Archbishop Mariano Rossell Arellano in the country. A pastoral letter, read out in all the churches (to a largely illiterate population) urged Guatemalans to 'rise up as one man against this enemy of God and country'. In Nicaragua, the Somozas – Anastasio ('Our Sonofabitch'), Luis and Anastasio Jr – all had the backing of the USA, and the Church. So did the murderous Contra Front after the Somoza tyranny was overthrown. In Honduras, Costa Rica – you name the country – the Church saw cruel conservative regimes as preferable to even moderately reforming ones. If Camilo Torres' claim that Christ would have been a leftist guerrilla must be questionable, it hardly seems likely that he would have joined a right-wing death-squad or a military *junta*.

In the days that followed, as police became increasingly suspicious that Calvi had been murdered, financial investigators found huge discrepancies in the Banco Ambrosiano's accounts. Accusations of malpractice had been flying around for years – Calvi himself had been convicted of illegally exporting currency and sentenced to four years' imprisonment, although he had been given his freedom while he waited to appeal. There were major fraud charges pending against him too. The day before his disappearance, his secretary had leapt from her fourth-floor office window, leaving a note alleging that her boss's crimes had brought the Banco Ambrosiano down. It was certainly in deep trouble, its management collectively dismissed by Italy's finance ministry, who had established their own committee to handle its affairs.

Right: Roberto Calvi served as President of the Banco Ambrosiano, Milan, until his suicide in 1982. His death drew unwelcome attention to the Vatican's extraordinarily intricate financial arrangements and exposed an unholy tangle of curious connections and secret deals.

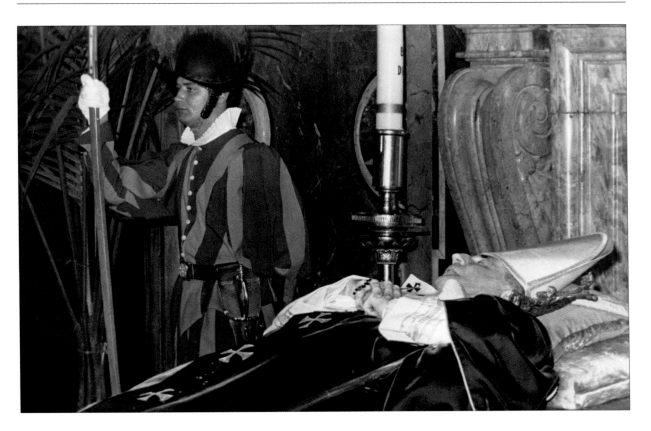

Above: John Paul I lies in state in the Clementine Chapel of St Peter's after the shortest papal reign of recent times. Inevitably, his death – after only 33 days in office – gave rise to rumour and speculation of the most lurid sort.

Calvi wasn't the first crooked financier, and he wouldn't be the last, but his was no ordinary story of corruption. As the chairman of the Banco Ambrosiano, he had become known as 'God's Banker', mainly because the Vatican Bank had owned a substantial shareholding. He had also been a prominent member of P2 – a masonic lodge that was rumoured to control the commanding heights of the Italian economy and media. (That P2 members jokily referred to themselves as the *frati neri* or 'black friars' – like the bridge – was said by some to have been a sign that his murder had been the work of his brother masons.)

What happened to Calvi isn't clear, and where a lack of clarity exists conspiracy theory thrives: speculation on the case has embraced everything from mafia money-laundering to channelling CIA funding to the Nicaraguan Contras. Archbishop Paul Marcinkus,

head of the Vatican Bank (or, in full, the 'Institute for the Works of Religion'), took a down-to-earth approach to this worldliest of duties: 'You can't run the Church on Hail Mary's', he observed. What Our Lady would have thought of his friendships (and, said his accusers, business dealings) with convicted fraudsters and international gangsters we can only guess.

Vatican Victim?

Was Pope John Paul I a collateral casualty of these shenanigans? Within 33 days of taking office he was dead. (Amazingly enough, that doesn't make his appointment by any means the shortest papal reign in history: in fact it comes in at number 11 in a table topped by Urban VII, whose reign in September 1590 had lasted only 13 days.) By the Vatican's own account his passing was just 'one of those things' – he was hardly the first man in his sixties to have had a heart attack. But speculation was inevitable: the peculiar combination of power, wealth and secrecy in the highest reaches of the Church make its affairs attractive to conspiracy theorists at the best of times – add in

FROM P2 TO PORN

THE CATHOLIC CHURCH has supped with so many devils down the centuries that one more won't make much difference, perhaps. Even so, it's curious to find such close and complex links between Catholic officials and Propaganda Due or 'P2', given the Church's longstanding opposition to freemasonry. (Since 1738, soon after the founding of the first Grand Lodges in Enlightenment Europe, the Church has banned its members from involvement in freemasonry.) Still, the converse should have been true as well. Born of the eighteenth-century Enlightenment, the 'Craft' had traditionally taken a contemptuous attitude towards the Church and its teachings. Instead, its members had espoused a 'deist' view in which a 'Grand Architect' had designed the universe.

Given the number of scandals, political and financial, in which the lodge's Venerable Master Licio Gelli was found to have been involved, it is hard to see him as a searcher of mystic truth. If the financier had any aim beyond that of enriching himself and his friends, it seems to have been the resurrection of Fascism in Italy – or at very least the extirpation of Communism in the country. This of course was an aim he shared both with the Catholic Church and the CIA, and with both organizations he seems to have maintained mysterious contacts down the years.

Gelli himself has withdrawn from the frontline of Italian politics in recent years: his plan for Italy's 'democratic rebirth' has been in good hands with Silvio Berlusconi, he has told the press. In backing Berlusconi's rise, the Church showed impressive tolerance in turning a blind eye to his TV empire's recipe of softcore imagery and right-wing propaganda. Its patience only snapped when the media mogul proved to have been getting too close to (allegedly under-age) girls himself at the 'bunga-bunga parties' to which he treated his friends.

Below: Pope John Paul II isn't sure he sees the joke he's supposed to share with Silvio Berlusconi. The Polish Pope had denounced the output of the billionaire media mogul's TV stations as a 'curse', but favoured the devil he knew over his liberal opponents.

Above: Scores were killed by a bomb in the Bologna Massacre of 1980. No one would suggest that the outrage was the work of the Church. But had senior Vatican officials allowed themselves to become too closely involved with those right-wing extremists who were responsible?

freemasonry and the recipe is irresistible. It would only take the addition of the CIA and KGB to make the mix complete – and both these elements have been added by investigative writers in the years since.

Of course, the fact that conspiracy theories flourish doesn't mean that there are no conspiracies, and what might loosely be described as the 'P2 Affair' had been a conspiracy and a half. While claims that the late Pope had paid the price for trying to break the hold of freemasons within his hierarchy or for seeking to stamp out corruption remain unproven, they can hardly be so easily dismissed. That there were illicit goings-on seems certain – even if their details have been difficult to delineate – while one would hesitate to say that certain elements would have stopped at murder. Prominent P2

members had kept coming up in investigations into the neo-fascist group that organized the Bologna Massacre in 1980 – a station bombing which left 85 people dead.

Il Papa and the Mamas

It hardly helped that the Vatican was so cagy in the days immediately following John Paul's death, even prevaricating over who had found the body – he had died in bed. The fear of salacious innuendo apparently prevented their revealing that his death had been discovered by his female housekeeper, Sister Vincenza Taffarel – a nun who had been brought in, cynics leered, at the request of the late Pope himself.

From 'cherchez la femme' to 'cherchez the feminist': some excitable commentators suggested that the Pope had fallen foul of traditionalists in his Church with his remark that 'God is Father, and, even more, He is Mother'. Most of those who read these words took them to mean, first, that God's love transcends mortal sex-roles, and, second, that he has a 'mother's' gentleness, but some took it to represent the embrace

of a revolutionary new gynotheology, replacing God with a Goddess. John Paul didn't live long enough to spell his meaning out.

In the Firing Line

John Paul I's successor, Poland's Cardinal Karol Wojtyła, paid him the compliment of taking his name as John Paul II. By contrast, his was to be one of the longest ever papacies. It was very nearly cut abruptly short, however, when, while riding in his 'popemobile' through a crowded St Peter's Square, on 13 May 1981, he was shot by Mehmet Ali Agca, a Turkish gunman. The Pope was critically injured but managed to survive.

John Paul II had become a figurehead for the freedom struggle throughout the Iron Curtain countries.

Ali Agca had a longstanding record as a member of Turkey's ultra-nationalist 'Grey Wolves' group – a quasi-fascist organization with a well-proven readiness to resort to murder when required. Despite his right-wing credentials, Agca's testimony to investigators after his arrest pointed to the involvement of the Bulgarian secret police, and hence in turn to that of their masters in the Soviet KGB, whose interest in seeing the Pope killed or incapacitated was all too clear. John Paul II had become a figurehead for the freedom struggle in his native Poland in particular, and in the Iron Curtain countries more generally.

John Paul subsequently went to see his would-be killer in prison, where he spoke to him 'as a brother', freely forgiving him for his attack. A plot by Islamic terrorists to deploy a suicide-bomber dressed as a priest against the Pope during a visit to the Philippines in 1995 was foiled when the plan was uncovered a few days before. Had it gone ahead, it was to have been followed up with the mass-hijacking of airliners en route from Asia to the United States – with a crash-attack on the CIA's Virginia headquarters rather like those against the World Trade Center and the Pentagon on 9/11.

Opposite: John Paul II visits his would-be-assassin Mehmet Ali Agca in prison in Rome.

MASS MURDERER?

JOHN PAUL II's ANTI-COMMUNIST credentials were unimpeachable, one might have thought. His small-c conservatism was also well attested. He was far more indulgent towards those who hankered after the old Latin liturgy of the 'Tridentine Mass' than either of his predecessors had been.

For some, though, he hadn't gone far enough. Followers of the French reactionary rebel Marcel Lefebvre weren't happy that he hadn't done more to rehabilitate their hero. Reviving the Tridentine Mass at the École Seminary he had founded near Fribourg, Switzerland, Lefebvre had started ordaining priests. Given that he had effectively established his own church-within-the-Church, it wasn't hard to see why the Vatican had been irked – or why even a sympathetic pope like John Paul II might have felt unable to give him more support.

Feelings ran high among the dissidents, and one – the Spanish priest Juan María Fernández y Krohn – went for the Pope with a bayonet during a visit to Portugal in 1982. In the event he failed to kill John Paul II. Afterwards he told his prosecutors that he had acted to save the Church: he believed that the Pope was a Soviet secret agent.

Ultra-traditionalist French Archbishop Marcel Lefebvre offered a real challenge, even to conservative leaders like John Paul II.

XI

NOT SO SAINTLY

Any institution that presumes to judge how people live is liable to be judged itself – and attract harsh criticism if seen to be falling short. The trust the Church has been accorded, its wealth and worldly power, have brought immense temptations – which haven't always been resisted.

◆

'You appear righteous to others, but within you are full of hypocrisy …'

For any Christian, the spectre of the scriptural Pharisee must loom large as a warning of how the appearance of goodness can militate against the reality. The holy hypocrite, following the letter of the law; judging petty transgressions; overvaluing respectability, but lacking the love and commitment that Christ demands … Jesus' complaint against the teachers who came to try and catch him out in Matthew 15:8 (see also Mark 7:6) echoes the complaint of Isaiah 29:13: 'These people honour me with their lips, but their hearts are far from me.' Christ was to be echoed in his turn in the words of Pope Francis in a sermon delivered at the Basilica of

Opposite: Pope Francis began his reign in March 2013 with a ready acknowledgement that he and his fellow-clergy had fallen badly short of the standards expected of them by their congregations – and by Christ. The Church's reputation had suffered badly in recent times.

St Paul's Outside the Walls, in Rome, just a few weeks after his election in 2013:

'Inconsistency on the part of pastors and the faithful between what they say and what they do, between word and manner of life, is undermining the Church's credibility. Those who listen to us and observe us must be able to see in our actions what they hear from our lips, and so give glory to God!'

How are even the humblest Catholics to encourage others to do right without – at least implicitly – suggesting that they know better and live better than they do themselves? And how are even good Catholics to maintain their Church's dignity when – as, inevitably must happen, human as they are – they fall short of the values they supposedly uphold? And if the best Catholics are prone to fail, what of those who may have more cynically and systematically exploited the power and trust their status in the Church has brought them to advance their careers and further their own selfish designs? Some critics would like us to see hypocrisy as being an essential component of Catholicism – it has certainly sometimes been a 'besetting sin'.

Above: Survivors of the Magdalene Laundries demonstrate outside Ireland's parliament in Dublin, demanding compensation for the thousands who slaved and suffered in what they believe was a lucrative operation.

It is an unfortunate stain on the reputation of an institution that has done (and continues to do) an enormous amount of good: the Catholic Church is the largest non-governmental provider of education and healthcare in the world. Heroic efforts, which have largely gone unsung. At times, though – and there have been far too many of these times – positions of power and authority have been abused. The trust earned by so many dedicated men and women has been exploited for vicious ends.

Dirty Linen

Yet even this sort of 'few bad apples' description doesn't cover the kind of harm that's done when an entire policy is built on unsound social and ethical foundations. Times change, of course, and attitudes with them, but it's hard to claim with any real conviction that, for example, the way the Magdalene Laundries were run was ever justified. These convent homes for 'fallen women' flourished in Ireland (and

elsewhere) from the early nineteenth century, and were not finally closed until late in the twentieth. Prison-like in their organization and punitive in their ethos, they subjected women to close confinement and a gruelling round of heavy, physical work. Over time, not just prostitutes but abused children and unmarried mothers – sent here by embarrassed families – were incarcerated. Former inmates testified to the sexual, physical and psychological abuse they had sustained in the homes.

Singer Sinéad O'Connor recalled that her own treatment had not been directly abusive (she had been given to the care of the nuns by an anxious father, concerned at 'problem' behaviour such as disobedience and petty theft). But she had been horrified to witness a friend's baby being torn from her arms, never to be seen again. And their confinement was cruel in itself. 'We were girls in there, not women, just children really,' she told the *Irish Sun*:

'And the girls in there cried every day. It was a prison. We didn't see our families, we were locked in, cut off from life, deprived of a normal childhood. We were told we were there because we were bad people. Some of the girls had been raped at home and not believed.'

> She got a thick string and she tied it round my neck for three days and three nights and I had to eat off the floor every morning.

Survivors described a regime in which they were stripped of their identity and forced into a self-effacing muteness: 'I walked up the steps that day', recalled Marina Gambold, in an interview with the BBC decades later, 'and the nun came out and said your name is changed, you are Fidelma, I went in and I was told I had to keep my silence ... I was working in the laundry from eight in the morning until about six in the evening. I was starving with the hunger, I was given bread and dripping for my breakfast every morning ... We had to scrub corridors, I used to cry with sore knees, housemaids' knees, I used to work all day in the laundry, doing the white coats and the pleating ...

'Punishments could be positively sadistic. "One day I broke a cup," Marina Gambold recalled, and the nun said, "I will teach you to be careful". She got a thick string and she tied it round my neck for three days and three nights and I had to eat off the floor every morning. Then I had to get down on my knees and I had to say, "I beg almighty God's pardon, Our Lady's pardon, my companions' pardon for the bad example I have shown."'

From 1922, at least, the Laundries

Left: A world away from the cruel drudgery of the Magdalene Laundry to which she was sent as a teenager, Sinéad O'Connor sings in Los Angeles, 2012. With her international profile, O'Connor has proven a powerful voice for a community of survivors whose complaints were silenced for so long.

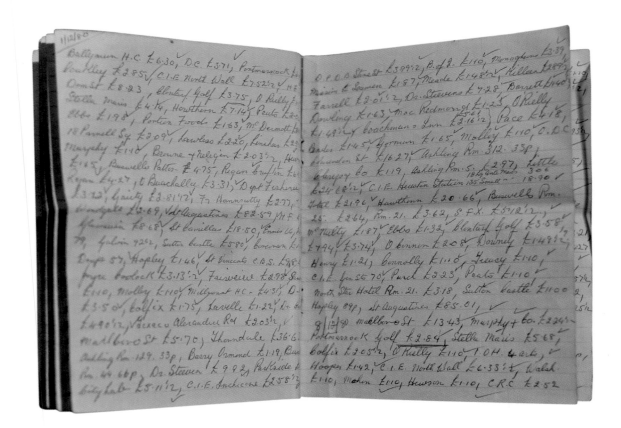

Above: A ledger from the Magdalene Laundry at Hyde Park, Dublin, gives a suggestion of the operation's scale. When the scandal broke, it became apparent that the Irish state had been an important client of a business protestors believe to have been a major moneymaker for the Church.

had operated under the auspices of an independent Ireland, many of their referrals – and their business contracts – being with the state. An official report compiled by former-senator Martin McAleese agreed that the institutions had been inhumane in their very ethos, but found no evidence to support survivors' claims of abuse. Or that, as many had been suggesting, the Church had made vast profits – however, McAleese concluded that the institutions had barely broken even. Critics have questioned his findings, however, pointing to the cursoriness of his enquiries into the Laundries' accounts and his officials' failure to discuss their treatment with survivors.

Hence the suspicions that the report was, if not actually a whitewash, at best a most half-hearted

investigation; hence too the scepticism about Taoiseach Enda Kenny's formal apology to survivors. While lamenting that the Laundries had been a 'national shame', he did so on the basis of a very limited acknowledgement of the scope of a scandal that remains controversial to this very day.

Today we wouldn't even recognize the concept of the 'fallen woman'; 'slut-shaming' is frowned-upon – however widespread it may be. And we'd recoil at the idea that a victim of child sex-abuse should suffer for another's sins. For some, such shifts in *zeitgeist* can be seen as accounting altogether for these crimes – if that's what they are: the nuns concerned (the Sisters of Mercy; the Good Shepherd Sisters; the Sisters of Charity and the Sisters of Our Lady of Charity) were guilty of nothing more than articulating the prejudices of their time. And up to a point, indeed, that's true: the state support the Magdalene Laundries were afforded would tend to bear this out. As does the existence of a comparable Protestant institution, the Bethany Home in Dublin, about which similar accusations have since

MONEY MAD

THERE CAN BE big money in poverty – especially where, as in the comparatively compassionate societies of the welfare age, charities can look to governments for financial backing. State funding appears to have been at issue when, in Canada's Quebec province in the 1940s, thousands of orphans in Church-run homes found themselves abruptly reclassified as mental patients. The reason for their recategorization appears to have been a change in the law determining that the care of orphans would thenceforth only receive provincial funding, while healthcare facilities would get funding from the Canadian government.

The 'Duplessis Orphans' – as they have been called, after the provincial premier of the time, Maurice Duplessis – arguably weren't even orphans (as the word is generally understood) to begin with. Most were the children of unmarried mothers, taken into the charge of the authorities. Suddenly, at the stroke of a pen, they were rebranded as mental patients. In addition to intrusive and sometimes painful 'psychiatric' treatments (which included everything from electroconvulsive therapy to lobotomy), many patients were later to complain of having been used as guinea pigs in medical experiments. Some experienced years of hardship, close confinement and physical and sexual abuse. Priests, nuns, psychiatrists and other staff all seem to have been implicated in mistreatment – as, indirectly, has the government of Quebec. In the face of a long and vociferous campaign, it has refused to hold an official inquiry and survivors have dismissed its offers of compensation as derisory.

Below: Sheet or shroud? This statue stands at the site of the old Sisters' of Mercy laundry in Galway City. Attempts have been made to have it moved somewhere less obtrusive: even now, this subject is a sore point for some in Ireland.

LOVE THY NEIGHBOUR?

OUTSIDE THE ENTRANCE on the Via Carducci, a set of male genitalia in exquisite topiary poked irreverent fun at the proprieties – and more-than-hinted at the delights to be found within.

For the Europa Multiclub in central Rome was the biggest gay bathhouse on the Continent – 'La Sauna Gay n°1', its publicity proclaimed. Punters could come to parties here to 'unleash' or simply relax in its Turkish bath and whirlpools; enjoy a massage; watch porn in company; hang out in a lounge or retire to a private room. Meanwhile, on the floor above, one of the Church's severest critics of homosexuality (or 'unnatural tendencies'), Cardinal Ivan Dias, had his 12-bedroom apartment. The Church in fact owned several properties in the same block, with a total value of £21 million.

The revelation embarrassed the Holy See just when the world's cardinals were gathering for the election that would bring about the elevation of Pope Francis in March 2013.

been made. This does, however, seem shaky ground on which to base the defence of a Church that has been so free with its exhortations to individual men and women to take moral responsibility for their actions.

Something Beautiful?

Ever since the British journalist Malcolm Muggeridge brought her to the world's attention with his documentary film *Something Beautiful for God* in 1969, Mother Teresa of Calcutta has been an icon. She died in 1997 and since 2003 has in the eyes of the Church been beatified as the 'Blessed Teresa' – she is halfway to sainthood, in other words. The founder, in 1950, of the Missionaries of Charity, her work in the city now known as Kolkata was deemed so inspiring that she was awarded the Nobel Peace Prize in 1979.

Emblematic of Catholicism's charitable mission in the modern world, she has at the same time inevitably been the test case by which the Church's claims to be a force for good have been assessed. And a great many of her critics have found her wanting. For all her ostentatious humility, this woman dedicated to the service of the 'poorest of the poor' seemed thoroughly at home among the rich and powerful, it was pointed out. And not just the powerful but the poisonous –

Opposite: Mother Teresa meets Pope John Paul II at the Vatican, 1997. The Albanian-born nun was a religious icon in her own lifetime. Like the Church she represented, though, she was dogged by controversy: her mission's methods were questionable; its finances obscure; many of her public pronouncements troubling.

> I saw children with their mouths gagged open to be given medicine, their hands flaying in distress, visible testimony to the pain they were in.

men like American Savings & Loan fraudster Charles Keating, whose donations she gratefully received (and refused to return for the benefit of his victims after his conviction), the corrupt British publisher Robert Maxwell and Haiti's cruel and kleptomaniac Duvaliers.

Meanwhile, it was hard for sceptics to see what the supposed beneficiaries of her saintly mission were actually gaining. Describing what he'd witnessed as an undercover observer making a documentary film in Mother Teresa's Calcutta mission, journalist and filmmaker Donal MacIntyre wrote in the *New Statesman* of disabled children being tied up to stop them straying. Conditions were generally Dickensian:

'I saw children with their mouths gagged open to be given medicine, their hands flaying in distress, visible testimony to the pain they were in. Tiny babies were bound with cloth at feeding time. Rough hands wrenched heads into position for feeding. Some of the children retched and coughed as rushed staff crammed food into their mouths. Boys and girls were abandoned on open toilets for up to 20 minutes at a time ...'

Volunteers, he said, did their best to clean those who'd soiled themselves:

'But there were no nappies, and only cold water. Soap and disinfectant were in short supply. Workers washed down beds with dirty water and dirty cloths. Food was prepared on the floor in the corridor. A senior member of staff mixed medicine with her hands.'

Heroic labours by selfless staff in impossible circumstances? Certainly, but why?, wondered MacIntyre. Thanks to extensive and uncritical coverage in the world media, contributions were flooding in to Mother Teresa's organization week by week, disillusioned former staff reported. The money went straight into international bank accounts.

This seems to have been at least in part a quasi-spiritual decision: God would provide for her patients, Mother Teresa reasoned; he would decide if someone lived or died. She doesn't seem to have believed in investment in modern healthcare technology – at least not for her charitable patients. (She herself had the best the world's prestigious hospitals could provide.) There was, she seems genuinely to have felt, something spiritually purifying in other people's suffering. She didn't even believe in administering painkillers: 'It is the most beautiful gift for a person,' she said, 'that he can participate in the sufferings of Christ.'

Of course, a fiercely spiritual Catholic and a secular liberal do come at questions of life and suffering from very different standpoints. Neither Mother Teresa nor her staff made any secret of their attitudes or showed the slightest shame at their 'exposure'. Which would seem to suggest a clear – if perhaps sadly misguided – conscience. It's difficult to avoid a certain sense of cognitive dissonance here when one finds that the Missionaries of Charity themselves actually welcomed what MacIntyre had intended as a damning documentary – apparently not even registering the critical message of the film. The late Christopher Hitchens, another critic, seems to have been as shocked as he was affronted when Mother Teresa's reaction to his polemical attack on her was insouciantly to 'forgive' him – regardless of whether or not he wanted that.

Right: Sisters of the Congregation Missionaries of Charity (Mother Teresa's order) process past a bank in Lucknow. An ironic image, given questions over the poor conditions of their patients, despite the donations to one of the most celebrated institutions in the world.

Sex AIDS

Something of the same mutual miscomprehension may be seen in secular society's disagreements with the Catholic Church over abortion: is the foetus a 'human life' or merely a cluster of cells? Those who hold the former position will naturally see abortion-

on-demand as a murderous 'holocaust' to be stopped at just about whatever cost – a wildly disproportionate reaction for those taking the latter view. The Church's prohibition on artificial forms of birth control is even more incomprehensible to outsiders (and to a great many Catholics in the developed world, where it's much ignored). Committed Catholics angrily reject the suggestion that they are in any sense 'anti-sex', although it's true that the rights and (mostly) wrongs of sex loom large in ethical debates within the Church. For many, the Church's arguments against contraception belong in the same philosophical realm

as the late Pope John Paul II's claim that a man could commit adultery with his wife: ingenious; perhaps even justified – yet fundamentally unconvincing.

If the Church's teaching on birth control is amusing to secular society in the West and exasperating to many Catholics, more serious objections are raised to anti-contraception campaigns in Africa. If we're going to talk about 'holocausts', what of the Church's attempts seemingly to sabotage the fight against AIDS in Africa, where more than a million adults and children die from the syndrome every year?

Catholic campaigns against the use of condoms have cost hundreds of thousands of lives (and counting) in Africa, it's been alleged. The Catholic counter-argument – that marital fidelity is best (and that condoms cost lives by encouraging risky behaviour) – is an argument that does not convince many secular commentators.

Reverend Romps
The Church's pious obduracy – if that's what it is – over all things sexual has been thrown into ironic

relief by the growing number of priests apparently struggling with their vows of chastity. Or, at least, with the difficulty of keeping their misdemeanors covered up: do we really have a more wayward clergy, or just a less compliant press? Sex scandals are nothing new, of course, but the 'permissive society' of the last few decades has arguably brought greater temptations for nuns and priests.

And, paradoxically, a greater readiness to judge on the part of a public which requires some convincing that clerical celibacy is either genuinely possible or desirable. We may have become slower to shock but we've been quicker to jeer – and arguably less tolerant than we were before. In an age when some degree of sexual repression was widespread, it may have been less difficult to imagine a refusal of sexual activity which didn't itself smack of sexual perversion. Today the choice immediately awakens a suspicion of hypocrisy, perhaps.

It is a suspicion that has been borne out by a succession of stories. Galway's Bishop Casey was found to have been carrying on with American divorcée Annie Murphy in 1992. They'd had a son together, the suddenly loquacious Murphy now revealed – the bishop had tried to get her to put him up for adoption, but she'd refused. Just four years later, Bishop Roderick Wright of Argyll and the Isles in Scotland ran off with Kathleen MacPhee in a humiliating flight from a delighted press, who subsequently learned that 'Roddy' had a 15-year-old son from an earlier romance as well. In 2012, the Bishop of Merlo Moreno, in Argentina,

Above: American divorcée Annie Murphy poses with Peter, the son she had in 1974 to Eamonn Casey – by the time the story broke the Bishop of Galway. His disgrace was an early humiliation for an Irish Church which was to see a lot more scandal in the years that followed.

Opposite: Is the Catholic Church doing the devil's work in southern Africa? Whilst its members battle valiantly against the ravages of AIDS, the hierarchy has been unbending on birth control. Campaigners question how HIV-infection can realistically be contained without the widescale use of barrier contraceptives.

was caught in compromising photos with a woman he tried to claim was a 'childhood friend'.

By this time, though, such comparatively conventional transgressions had come to seem a lot less compelling to the watching media. In 2005, another Argentinian bishop, Juan Carlos Maccarone, had been precipitated into early retirement by the surfacing of a film that showed him engaging in sexual acts with a 23-year-old man. Four years later, across the River Plate in Uruguay, Bishop Francisco Domingo Barbosa Da Silveira resigned after it was alleged he'd broken his vow of celibacy. Edinburgh's

Opposite: Cheerful, brisk and businesslike, Cardinal Keith Patrick O'Brien cuts an impressive figure as he strides across St Peter's Square in 2005. Less than a decade later he was in disgrace, his well-publicized attacks on gay marriage undermined by his admission of having 'fallen short' in his own behaviour.

Above: As a cardinal, Joseph Ratzinger had been described, half-fearfully, half-admiringly as 'God's Rottweiler', but he proved much meeker as Pope Benedict XVI. His early abdication is still a mystery: Benedict's health had not been great, but some hinted darkly at political intriguing behind the scenes.

Cardinal Keith Patrick O'Brien, who in November 2012 had been awarded the title 'Bigot of the Year' by gay rights charity Stonewall for his condemnation of civil partnerships, gay marriage and – ultimately – anything that might 'facilitate or promote' same-sex relationships, was forced to step down a few months later over allegations of inappropriate approaches to younger priests. He subsequently admitted that there had been 'times' when his sexual conduct had 'fallen short of the standards expected' of him – and not just in his younger days as a priest but in more recent years 'as … archbishop and cardinal'.

PERSONA NUN GRATA

Sister Simone Campbell wowed the Democratic National Convention in 2012 with an impassioned plea for progress on ObamaCare (the Affordable Care Act). But the social justice campaigner, who had cut her teeth as a community lawyer, hadn't been such a hit with the hierarchy back in Rome. Sister Simone was regarded as ringleader of a group of American nuns who'd embarrassed both rightwing Republicans and the Church with their outspoken comments on social questions – and their alleged failure to condemn contraception, abortion and same-sex marriage with sufficient force.

'GIVE ME A CHILD...'

A vast and powerful institution, wily in the ways of the world, the Church has seen scandals come and go over 2000 years – but can it so easily shrug off the problems which beset it now?

◆

'Let the children come to me, and do not hinder them.' – MATTHEW 19: 14

'Give me a child until he is seven, and I'll give you the man.' The saying is famously attributed to the Jesuits. Unfortunately, it's come to ring so true in such a shockingly unpalatable way that increasingly few parents these days would feel entirely easy trusting any member of the Catholic clergy with their child. Throughout the 1990s the stories came streaming in of physical brutality and – even more disturbing – sexual abuse in countless orphanages, schools and other institutions, all continuing unchecked over several decades.

Gradually, the realization grew that abuse had been brutal and widespread, that it had involved just about every area of Church life and every religious order, and that in some contexts it hadn't been just

Opposite: Anti-child abuse protesters march with placades in London during the state visit to Britain of Pope Benedict XVI, September 2010. Many critics believed that the Catholic Church were aware of abuse in its institutions but failed to act.

frequent but systemic. In Ireland, for example, the Christian Brothers topped the table for brutality and sexual abuse; reported cases from their homes in other countries, from Canada to Australia, ran into thousands.

While the perpetrators were individual priests, brothers and nuns, the hierarchy as a whole was implicated – and not just in the technical sense of being responsible for what had happened 'on its watch'. For, time and again, it turned out that victims had tried to speak up, to take their complaints to the Church authorities, only to find themselves flatly ignored – or pressured into silence. The backlash was slow in coming, but devastating once it arrived: child-abuse payouts have bankrupted no fewer than eight US dioceses in the past 20 years.

A Nasty Nazareth

For most lay Catholics – and observers outside the Church – the most shocking thing about the abuse scandals was the unimaginable mismatch between what was being reported and the saintly public image of those involved. Critics who were quick to see corruption and cynicism in the Church's hierarchy

Above: An alleged victim of child abuse collapses in distress after being interviewed at a Dublin demonstration. The Church's systematic cynicism in covering up such practices has badly damaged its reputation in an Ireland which always looked on its Catholic clergy with love and trust.

didn't question the commitment of ordinary priests and nuns. And how could they? These men and women had given up the good things in life for the service of others. They lived poorly and simply – that was plain for all to see.

But did they, wondered some of those they 'helped', take the deprivations of their own lives out of others? 'Looking back,' one former inmate of a Nazareth home told the *Independent on Sunday* (16 August 1998), 'I think one of the reasons was that the nuns weren't happy and they decided we damn well weren't going to be either.'

And they duly damn well weren't. Vera Willshire, who lived in the Nazareth Sisters' home in Middlesbrough, northern England, described a regime of unrelenting brutality. 'I was terrified the whole time and never had a happy day', she said. Once in particular, she reported, she had been 'beaten black and blue, so badly I had to stay in the infirmary for five weeks. When I came out I was given a bag of sweets and told to tell no one about what happened. An aunt who came to visit was told I was confined with an infection.'

Bedwetting, Vera said, 'was about the worst thing you could do. The punishment was being forced to stand in front of a nun's cell with the soiled linen on your head or being sat in the galvanized steel bath while two assistants poured buckets of cold water over your head.'

Of course, the more frightened and traumatized children were, the more they wet their bed. Commissioned by the government of Queensland to look into abuse accusations against the sisters in that state, Professor Bruce Grundy found evidence of 'ruthless and sadistic madness' among the nuns.

Below: Brendan Smyth, the paedophile-priest, leaves Limavady courthouse after being extradited to the Irish Republic to face charges in 1994. He is believed to have molested well over 100 children in his time, shielded from justice by the hierarchy of the Church.

> The punishment was being forced to stand in front of a nun's cell with the soiled linen on your head or being sat in the galvanized steel bath while two assistants poured buckets of cold water over your head.

Priest and Paedophile

Among the most notorious cases was that of Belfast-born Father Brendan Smyth. Between the 1940s and 1990s, he molested over 100 children. His victims included both boys and girls in a succession of parishes, first in his home city and then in Dublin and in various parts of the United States. His superiors in the Norbertine order, although well aware of his proclivities from early on, contrived to conceal

his crimes. Rather than reporting him, they moved him on from parish to parish – where each time he was welcomed by unsuspecting churchgoers, old and young. The wider Church was implicated, the hierarchy having repeatedly turned a deaf ear to complaints by one of Father Smyth's Norbertine colleagues.

By the 1970s, the offences still continuing, further action had to be taken. Two teenage boys with complaints against the priest were allowed to bring them forward at a special hearing at their school, St Patrick's College, Cavan – but then bullied into signing oaths of silence on the matter. Smyth was free to re-offend – and his superiors to continue with their cover-up. Father Smyth was finally arrested in 1991 in Northern Ireland but jumped bail and spent three years as a fugitive in the Republic. (The widespread suspicion that the Fianna Fáil–Labour government there was deliberately obstructing an extradition request from the authorities in the North caused deep disgust and, eventually, the coalition's fall.) Finally, having served three years in Ulster's Magilligan prison, he was taken to the Curragh Prison, outside Dublin, where – a year into a 12-year sentence – he collapsed and died.

Only after this did Cardinal Seán Brady, Archbishop of Armagh and Primate of All Ireland, admit that – as a young priest and professor at St Patrick's – he himself had been among those present at the 1975 tribunal. He claimed that he had seen no reason to bring the case to the attention of the secular authorities. No action was taken against him by the Catholic Church even then, although for many months that followed he was forced to dodge doorstepping reporters outside his Dublin residence. As of the autumn of 2013, indeed, he remains in office.

For the Church's critics, the bland complacency of the hierarchy has been as shocking as the abuse itself. The cliché has it that the cover-up is worse than the crime, but here in truth it's hard to tell the two apart. By conspiring to conceal those sexual assaults that were brought to its attention, the Church allowed further offences to take place. More than that, it arguably encouraged them: the policy of moving a paedophile priest on to a new parish once he'd been reported guaranteed him a fresh flock where no one could have been forewarned.

A New Persecution?

Has the Church had an unfair press? Its most indefatigable supporters would like us to think so – although, even among avowed Catholics, such defenders are comparatively few and far between. There *is* a case, if not for the defence, at least for the suggestion that the Church has by no means been uniquely at fault in protecting child abuse, and that it certainly hasn't been as bad as it's sometimes been painted. The last few decades have seen accusations of sexual abuse from a bewildering range of different state-run and private institutions, from playgroups and remand homes to youth sports teams and the

THE POPE AND THE PULITZER

THE SCANDAL OF clerical child abuse may well be as old as the Church, and there's no particular reason to assume it's been worse in one place than it has been in another. That the story first broke in the United States was perhaps inevitable, though: loyal Catholic commentators were to blame that country's tirelessly inquisitive, irreverent media, and its traditions of public litigiousness and anti-Catholicism for the furore surrounding a series of exposés in the *Boston Globe* in 2002.

In doing so, they were clearly blaming the symptoms rather than the cause, but there's no doubt that the American media and political culture was one in which all these things were present. It was, moreover, a culture in which a public apology and a show of breast-beating has been shown to work wonders, but this wasn't the Catholic Church's way of doing things. Instead, the Vatican greeted the Globe's revelations – rewarded with a Pulitzer Prize – with a stubborn silence.

Above: Activists in Los Angeles hold up quilts decorated with pictures of those who suffered sexual abuse at the hands of the city's priests. Despite paying out over $600 million in compensation, critics claim the archdiocese is concealing other Incriminating documents.

BBC. Have Catholic homes and schools been so different? And have priests been so much worse? Men in positions of authority – from the Church to the judiciary, taking in teachers, the police and the medical profession – have historically been prone to take advantage of their power. The risks of abuse are enormous – and enhanced by the tendency of the institutions within which all these abusers work to see off threats to their prestige by closing ranks and covering up.

There may well be a degree of truth in the suggestion that the relative scale of the Church's problems have been exaggerated – mythologized even. Certainly, the institution itself seems awesome and mysterious in the context of a non-Catholic culture – an effect intensified by its own resistance to any sort of transparency. Even Catholics feel that, as individuals, they're at the periphery of an unimaginably far-reaching organization: it's hard to imagine a *Da Vinci Code* set among Anglicans or Reform Jews. In one sense it may have suited the Church that neither Pope John Paul II nor Benedict XVI were ever directly and definitively implicated in the scandal – but in the absence of a clear chain of accountability, they couldn't convincingly be cleared either. At the same time, as vast as it is, the Church seems monolithic; easy to identify (and, consequently, sue), whereas the word 'Protestantism' represents any number of independent churches and tiny sects.

Promise to Protect

Pledge to Heal

BP GREGORY   ABP FLYNN   ABP DOLAN

Losing Faith

Whatever the reason, the mud has stuck. As early as 2002, 64 per cent of those responding to a poll commissioned by the *Wall Street Journal* and NBC News were agreeing that Catholic priests abused children 'frequently'. This despite the fact that a range of authoritative US bodies – from children's charities to the insurance industry – could find no significant difference in the rate of abuse between priests and Protestant clergy (or comparable figures, such as rabbis). Nor, according to more rigorous surveys (most notably one by the independent researchers of Philadelphia's John Jay Institute), was there any difference between the rate of offending between the Catholic Clergy and men in general.

Just how reassuring should we find this, though? Shouldn't Catholic priests be *better* than men in

Above: When trust goes, it goes completely, Bishop Wilton Gregory (left) finds, addressing an incredulous press corps for the US Conference of Catholic Bishops.

general? Don't such defences rest on precisely the sort of 'moral relativism' the Church and its supporters are supposed to scorn?

And, granting that Christ asked us to love the sinner, would he have wanted his legacy on Earth to be an institution which, by covering up for him, connived in the sinner's crimes? And which, by its systematic refusal to examine its collective conscience, let evil thrive and suffering continue among the innocent and vulnerable children in its charge. 'Truly I tell you,' Christ was to remind his disciples in Matthew (25: 31), 'Whatever you did to the least of my brothers, you did to me.'

THE EMBITTERED ISLE

BACK IN 1984, it is estimated, 90 per cent of Ireland's people regularly went to mass. If you chose not to, you were regarded with suspicion. By 2011, in contrast, only an ageing 18 per cent were regular attenders. Now, it seemed, the stigma was attached to going. An international poll of 2012 found fewer than half of its Irish respondents prepared to describe themselves as 'religious' – 47 per cent, compared to 69 per cent just seven years earlier.

How far the blame for this precipitous decline can be lain at the doorstep of Father Smyth's presbytery or Cardinal Brady's residence is hard to know for sure: we should be wary of reading too much into anecdotal evidence, however vivid. Church attendance has been declining across the Western world for many years, a function (arguably) of everything from expanding education to televised football, from changing family structures to DIY. Apathy is one thing, though; outspoken atheism another: Ireland is now among the world's most godless countries. Ten per cent of the population were prepared to describe themselves as 'convinced atheists'. Again, the contrast with the situation just seven years earlier was stark – then only three per cent would have claimed this status.

Few commentators doubt that the child-abuse scandal has transformed attitudes to the Church in what was once the world's 'most Catholic country'.

Below: Pope Benedict XVI addresses an emergency meeting of senior Irish clergy at the Vatican in the wake of an ever-growing and seemingly never-ending child-abuse scandal which had thrown this most Catholic of countries into a deep crisis of faith.

BIBLIOGRAPHY

Books

Abulafia, David. *The Discovery of Mankind: Atlantic Encounters in the Age of Columbus.* London: Yale University Press, 2010.

Ansary, Tamim. *Destiny Disrupted: A History of the World Through Islamic Eyes.* New York: PublicAffairs, 2010.

Asbridge, Thomas. *The Crusades: The War for the Holy Land.* London: Simon & Schuster, 2010.

Casanova, Julián. *The Spanish Republic and Civil War.* London: I.B. Tauris, 2010.

Collins, Roger. *Keepers of the Keys of Heaven: A History of the Papacy.* London: Weidenfeld & Nicolson, 2009.

Duffy, Eamon. *Saints and Sinners: A History of the Popes.* London: Yale University Press, 2006.

Ferriter, Diarmaid. *Occasions of Sin: Sex and Society in Modern Ireland.* London: Profile, 2012.

Green, Toby. *Inquisition: The Reign of Fear.* London: Macmillan, 2007.

Kennedy, Hugh. *The Great Arab Conquests: How the Spread of Islam Changed the World We Live In.* London: Weidenfeld & Nicolson, 2007.

Lewis, Brenda Ralph. *The Popes: A Dark History.* London: Amber, 2009.

Maalouf, Amin, tr. Rothschild, J. *The Crusades through Arab Eyes.* London: Saqi, 1984.

MacCullough, Diarmaid. *Reformation: Europe's House Divided, 1490–1700.* London: Allen Lane, 2003.

_____. *A History of Christianity: The First 3,000 Years.* London: Allen Lane, 2009.

Meyer, Michael C. and Beezley, William. eds. *The Oxford History of Mexico.* New York: OUP USA, 2000.

Murphy, Cullen. *God's Jury: The Inquisition and the Making of the Modern World.* London: Penguin, 2013.

Norwich, John Julius. *The Popes: A History.* London: Vintage, 2012.

Phillips, Charles, Budzik, Mary and Kerrigan, Michael. *The Illustrated Encyclopedia of Catholicism: A Comprehensive Guide to the History, Philosophy and Practice of Catholic Christianity.* London: Lorenz, 2009.

Phillips, Jonathan. *The Fourth Crusade and the Sack of Constantinople.* London: Cape, 2004.

Riley-Smith, Jonathan. *The Oxford History of the Crusades.* Oxford: OUP, 2002.

Websites

New Advent: The Catholic Encyclopedia, http://www.newadvent.org/cathen/

INDEX

References to illustrations are shown in *italics*.

A

abortion 204–5
Adrianople 28
Africa
  AIDS 206, *206*
  and Augustine 31
  and birth control 206
  Congo Free State 166, 168, *168*
  missionaries 121, 123, *123*, 148,
    166–9, *167*, *168*, *169*
  and Muslims 32, *33*
  slavery 121, 123
Agca, Mehmet Ali *194*, 195
AIDS 206, *206*
al-Andalus 33, 103
Albert of Aix 40–1, 43, 44
Albigensian Crusade 50, 52
Alexander VI, Pope 121, *122*, 124,
  124–5, 127–9, *128–9*
Alexius I, Byzantine Emperor 38, 41
Ambrose, Saint 65, *67*
Americas
  missionaries 155–60
  slavery 123
  see also individual countries
Andalucía 33, 103
Anglicanism 138, 141, 142
anti-Popes 65, 76–7, *78*, *79*, *79*
anti-Semitism *see* Jews
anticlericalism 173–5
Antioch *42*, 43, 47
apostasy 23, 25, 31
Aragón 70
archives, Vatican 13, *13*
Argentina 186, *186*, 187, 207
Arianism 31, 65–6
Arius 65–6
Arouet, François-Marie *see* Voltaire
Asia, and missionaries 149, 151–4
Assyrian Church 66
Augustine, Saint 9, 27 (quote), 28, *29*,
  30, 31, 32
auto da fé *92*, 97, *100–1*, 101, 103
Avignon 70, *72–3*, 73, 75, 76–9
Aztecs 159, *160*

B

Bale, John 117, *117*
Banco Ambrosiano 188, 190–1
Baret, John 88
Beckett, St Thomas 88
Belgium 166–8
Benedict, Sister Marie *12*
Benedict XIII, anti-Pope 76, *78*, 79, *79*
Benedict XVI, Pope *209*, 215, *217*
Benjamin, Thomas 173
Bergoglio, Jorge *see* Francis, Pope
Berlusconi, Silvio 192, *192*
Bernard of Clairvaux, Saint *45*
Berruguete, Pedro *92*
Béziers *50*, *51*, 52
birth control 205–6
Blood Libel 22, 53
Bohemia 58
Bohemund of Tarent 43
Bologna Massacre 193, *193*
Boniface III, Pope 70
Boniface VIII, Pope 85, 86, *86*
books, banned 111
Borgia family 121–9, *122*, *124–5*, *126*,
  128–9
Borgia, Lucrezia *126*, 127–8, *128–9*
Borgia, Rodrigo *see* Alexander VI, Pope
Bosch, Hieronymus *83*
Boston Globe 214
Bouts, Aelbert *14*
Brady, Cardinal Seán 214
Broz, Josip (Marshal Tito) *170*, 171
Byron, Lord *10*
Byzantium 38

C

Calles Law 173–4
Callixtus I, Pope 65, *65*
Callixtus III, Pope 121
Calvi, Roberto 188, *190*, 190–1
Calvin, John 137
Campbell, Sister Simone 209
Canada, Duplessis Orphans 201
Candide (Voltaire) 146
cannibalism, Crusades 43–4
Canterbury Cathedral 88
Canterbury Tales 88, 89

Carolus Magnus 68, *68*
Caron, Antoine *140*
Casey, Bishop Eamonn 207, *207*
catacombs 21, 23
Catharism 49–50, *51*
Celestine V, Pope 70, *71*
celibacy 115, 118, 207–9
censorship 111
Central America 187, *188–9*, 190
charity funding 201
Charlemagne 68, *68*
Charles I of Spain 161, *161*
Charles II of Sicily and Naples 70
Charles V, Holy Roman Emperor 133
Charles V of France 76
Charles VIII of France 129
Chaucer, Geoffrey 88, 89
child abuse 210–17
Chile 184, 186, *187*
China 149, 151
Choniates, Nicetas 69
Christian Brothers 211
Christian Martyr's Last Prayer, The 21
Church of England 138, 141, 143
Church Suffering 87
CIA 190
City of God, The (St Augustine) *30*, 31
Clement V, Pope 70, 73, 75
Clement VI, Pope *84*, 88
Clement VII, Pope 133
Clermont, Council of *39*
Cocks, Richard 154
Coligny, Admiral de 143
Cologne 40
Colonna family 70
Columbus, Christopher *109*
communism 171, 181–2, 184, 187
*Compilation of Instructions for the Office of
  the Holy Inquisition* 106, *106*
Concordat of Worms (1122) 90
Congo Free State 166, *167*, 168, *168*
Constantine 23, 25, 27
Constantinople 38, 41, 66, 68–9
contraception 205–6
Copernicus, Nicolaus 111
Cornelius, Pope 65
Cortés, Hernán *158*, 159–60

Court of the Inquisition, A 99
Courtenay, William, Bishop of London 56
Cromwell, Thomas 140
crucifixion *14*, 16, *19*
Crusader States 44, 47
Crusades *40*, *41*
  Albigensian Crusade 50, 52
  and Antioch *42*, 43, 47
  background to 37–8, *39*
  Constantinople 69
  Fifth Crusade *148*
  First Crusade 38–47
  Fourth Crusade 49, 69
  and France 38, 40, *46*–7, 49–50, *50*, *51*, 52
  and Jerusalem 44, *44*
  and Jews 38, 40–1, 44, 52–4, *53*
  and Ma'ara 43–4
  and Muslims 47, 49, 54
  Northern Crusades 54–5, 57
  People's Crusade 38–47
  Prussian Crusade 55, 57
  Second Crusade *45*, *46*–7
  Syria 41–3, 49
  Teutonic Knights 55, *55*, 57
  Third Crusade 47, 49
  and Urban II, Pope *36*, 37–8, *39*
Cuba 156
Cyprian, Bishop of Carthage *64*

D

Damned by the Inquisition 107
Dante 90, *91*
de Mailly, Jean 66
de' Medici family *112*, 113, 115, 127
  Clement VII, Pope 133
  Leo X, Pope 131–2, 135, 137, 138
de Mendoza, Maria 108
deism 146
Descartes, René 145, *145*
Diderot, Denis 146
Diocletian, Emperor 19–20, *20*, 25
Dominic de Guzman, Saint *92*
Dominican Republic 190
Donation of Constantine 25
Donatists 31
Duplessis Orphans 201

E

East-West schism 67–9
Edict Against the Christians 20

Edict of Toleration 25
Egypt, Crusades *148*
El Salvador 187, *188*–9
Elizabeth I, Queen of England 143
England
  child abuse 212–13
  and indulgences 87–8
  and Joan of Arc 58
  relics 88–9
  Reformation 138–43
Enlightenment 145–7
Erasmus, Desiderius 137
Eusebius 20

F

fascism 175–6, 192, 195
factionalism 63–79
Farnese, Giulia della 128
Felix, Minucius 22
Ferdinand of Spain 102, *102*, *103*, 105, 106
Fifth Crusade *148*
First Crusade 38–47
First Vatican Council *164*–5, 165–6
Florence 113, 115, 117, 120
Fourth Crusade 69
France
  Catharism 49–50, *51*
  Charles V of France 76
  Charles VIII of France 129
  and the Crusades 38, 40, *46*–7, 49–50, *50*, *51*, 52
  deism 146
  Enlightenment 145–6
  French wars of religion 143
  heretics 10, 57, 58, *60*
  and the Inquisition 94
  Jansenism 10
  Joan of Arc 58, *60*
  Lefebvre, Marcel 195, *195*
  Louis VII of France *46*–7
  Muslim occupation 32–3
  Philip IV of France 70, *74*, 75
  Popes and anti-Popes 70, *72*–3, 73, 75, 76–9
  Protestantism *142*, 143
  Reformation 143
Franceschetto (son of Innocent VIII) 120
Francis of Assisi, Saint *98*, *148*
Francis, Pope 186, 187, *196*, 197

Francis Xavier, Saint *150*, 151, 153, *153*
Franciscans, missionaries 151
Franco, Francisco 176, *178*, 179
Fraternité de Notre Dame *12*
fraud 190–1
freemasonry 191, 192, 193
Fulcher of Chartres 44

G

Galerius 25
Galilei, Galileo *110*, 111
Gambold, Marina 199
Gelli, Licio 192
gematria 20
Germany
  and the Crusades 40–1, *48*, 55, *55*, 57
  and Hitler, Adolf 179–81
  and the Reformation 143–5
Gérôme, Jean-Léon *21*
Gibbon, Edward 77
Girolamo 117
Giusti, Monsignor Martino *13*
Goa 153
Godfrey of Bouillon 40, 44
Goths 28
Granada 105
Grand Inquisitor 106
Great Persecution 19–21, 25
Gregory the Great, Pope 85
Gregory VII, Pope *89*, 90
Gregory XI, Pope 76
Gregory, Wilton *216*
Grossgmain, Master of *29*
Guadalete *33*
Guatemala 190
Guicciardini 127
guilt 10, 11
Guise, Duke of 143
Gundlach, Gustav 181
Gutiérrez, Gustavo 187, *188*

H

Hammer of Wrongdoers 61, *61*
Helena, Saint *80*
hell *30*, 31, 83, 90, *91*
Henri III of Navarre 143
Henricus Institoris 61
Henry III, King of England 87–8
Henry IV, Holy Roman Emperor *89*, 90

Henry VI, King of England 58
Henry VIII, King of England 138, *139,*
 140, 140–1
heretics
  and Augustine 32
  auto da fé *92, 97, 100–1, 101,* 103
  Copernicus, Nicolaus 111
  and the Crusades 50, *51,* 52
  Galilei, Galileo 111
  Hus, Jan 58, *59*
  and the Inquisition 93–111
  Jansenism 10
  Joan of Arc 58, *60*
  Nestorian Schism 66
  Tyndale, William 137
  Wycliffe, John *56,* 57
heterodoxy 58
Hideyoshi, Toyotomi 152
Hindus 153
Hispaniola 155–6
Hitler, Adolf 179–81
Holocaust 181
Holy Roman Empire, creation of 68
homosexuality 117, 203, 209
Huguenots *142,* 143
Hus, Jan 58, *59*
Hussites 58

I
Iberia 32, 49
Ice, Battle of the (1242) *55*
Incas *156–7*
Independent on Sunday 212
Index, The 111
India 6, 151, 153
indulgences 85–8, *87,* 137
infallibility, papal 165–6
Infessura, Stefano 117
Innocent III, Pope 49, *52*
Innocent IV, Pope 87–8, *98*
Innocent VIII, Pope 118–19, 120, *121*
Inquisition 93–111
  auto da fé *92, 97, 100–1, 101,* 103
  Grand Inquisitor 106, *106*
  the Inquisitors 96, 97, 98, 101, 102,
   106
  and Italy 109–11, *110*
  and the New World 108–9
  and pure-bloodedness 105–6
  and Spain 93–103, 105–9
  Torquemada 102
  torture 93–4, 97–9, *97, 98, 99,* 106

Investiture Contest 90
Ireland
  child abuse 213–14
  church attendance 217
  guilt 10
  Magdalene Laundries 198–200
  Pope's visit (John Paul II) *11*
Isabella of Spain 102, *102, 103,* 105,
 106
Islam *see* Muslims
Italy
  Bologna Massacre 193, *193*
  fascism 175–6
  Florence 113, 115, 117, 120
  and guilt 10
  and the Inquisition 109–11, *110*
  Michelangelo *136*
  Mussolini, Benito 175–6, *176*
  Naples 70
  Pazzi Conspiracy *112,* 113, 115, 117
  Popes and anti-Popes 65, 70, 75–6
  Resurgence 165
  Siena cathedral *130–1*
  St Peter's basilica 135, 137
  see also de' Medici family; Roman
   Empire; Rome; Vatican

J
Jansen, Cornelius 10
Japan 152, 154, *154*
Jaruzelski, Gen Wojciech 182, *184*
Jerusalem
  and the Crusades 38, 44, *44,* 47
  and the Knights Templar 75
  pilgrimage to 38
Jesuits 151, *155*
Jesus, central tenets 20
Jews
  and Benedict XIII, Pope 79
  Blood Libel 22, 53
  and the Crusades 38, 40–1, 44, 52–4,
   53
  as 'killers of Christ' 40, 53
  and Muslims 32
  and Nazis 180–1
  and Pius IX, Pope 166
  and Pius XII, Pope 181
  and pure-bloodedness 106
  as scapegoats 40, 53
  in Spain 79, 105, 106, 109
  in twentieth century 181
Joan of Arc 58, *60*

Joan, Pope 66, *66*
John XXIII, anti-Pope 77, *77*
John Paul I, Pope 191, *191,* 193
John Paul II, Pope *11, 184, 202*
  assassination attempts *194,* 195
  and Berlusconi, Silvio 192, *192*
  and child abuse scandals 215
  and communism 187–8, 195
  and contraception 206
  and Liberation Theology 187–8
  and Poland 182, *182–3*
jubilees 85, 86
judgment, final 83, *83,* 85
Julius II, Pope *116,* 128–9, 131, *132,*
 135, *136,* 137

K
Knights Templar 75
Knights, Teutonic 55, *55,* 57

L
Las Casas, Bartolomè de 155–6, 161,
 161
Last Judgement, The 83
Lateran Treaty 175
Latvia *54,* 55
Lefebvre, Marcel 195, *195*
Leo X, Pope 131–2, 135, 137, 138
Leopold II, King of Belgium 166, *167,*
 168
Leyenda Negra 94, 97
Liberation Theology 187
limpieza de sangre 105–6, *105*
Lithgow, William 93–4, *95*
Lithuania 55, 57
Lollards 57
Louis VII of France *46–7*
Luther, Martin *134,* 137

M
Ma'ara 43–4
MacIntyre, Donal 203–4
Magdalene Laundries 198–200, *198,*
 199, 200, 201
Magnasco, Alessandro *99*
Malleus Maleficarum 61, *61*
Marcinkus, Paul 191
Marguerite of Valois 143
Marranos 109
Martel, Charles 32–3, *34*
martyrdom of objects 179

martyrs
    early 15–16, 19, 20–1, *21*
    in Japan 152, 154, *154*
    in the Reformation 141, *141*, 143
Mary I, Queen of England 141, 143
Mass of Bolsena 132
McAleese, Martin 200
Mecca 32
Medici family 113, 115, 117, 131–2,
    133
Medjugorje 171, *172–3*, 173
Mexico 159, 173–4
Michelangelo *136*
Milvian Bridge, Battle of (312) *23*, 25
missionaries
    in Africa 121, 123, *123*, *148*, 166–9,
        167, *168*, *169*
    in the Americas 155–61
    in China 149, 151
    in Hispaniola 155–6
    in India 151, 153
    in Japan 152, 154, *154*
    in Mexico 156, 158–60
    in the New World 155–62
    Requirement, the 160, 162
Missionaries of Charity, Kolkata 6,
    203–4, *204–5*
Moctezuma 159, *159*
Mola, Gen Emilio 179
money
    funding for charities 201
    and indulgences 85–8, *87*, 137
    and Leo X, Pope 135, 137
    from salvation 86–8, *87*, 88–90
    from relics 88–90
    from simony 90, *91*
    Vatican Bank 188, 190–1
Monophysitism 66
Moors 32–3, 93, 109
More, Thomas 140, *140*
Moriscos 109
Mortara, Edgardo 166
Mother Teresa 7, *202*, 203–4
Muggeridge, Malcolm 203
Muhammad 31–2
Muhammad II of Granada *103*
Murphy, Annie 207, *207*
Muslims
    and the Crusades 47, 49, 54
    early battles with Christianity
        31–5, *34*

in France 32–3
and John Paul II, Pope 195
Muhammad 31–2
and pure-bloodedness 106
Saladin 47, 49, *49*
in Spain 53, 103, 105, 106, 108, 109
Mussolini, Benito 175–6, *176*
Mwanga II, King of Buganda 168

N
Nagasaki 152, 154, *154*
Naples 70
Nazis 180–1
nepotism 115
Nero, Emperor 16, 19
Nestorian Schism 66
Netherlands, Reformation 143
New Statesman 203–4
New World, and missionaries 155–61
Newton, Isaac 145, *146*
Nicaragua 187, 190
Nicholas IV, Pope 70, *70*, 149
Norbertine order 213–14
Northern Crusades 54–5, 57
Norwich 53
numerology 20, *20*
Nuremberg Chronicle 22

O
ObamaCare 209
O'Brien, Cardinal Keith Patrick *208*,
    209
O'Connor, Sinead 198–9, *199*
original sin 10, 31
Outrage, the 70

P
P2 191, 192, 193
Pacelli, Eugenio *180*, 181
Pagans 20, 23, 25, 44, 54
papal infallibility 165–6
Pardoner (Chaucer's) 88, 89
pardons *see* indulgences
Passover *22*
Paul, Saint 15–16, *18*, 32, *62*
Pazzi *112*, 113, 115
Pazzi Conspiracy *112*, 113, 115, 117
Pelagius 31
People's Crusade 38–47
persecution, early Roman Empire
    20–1, 25

Peru *156–7*
Peter, Saint 16, *19*, 23, 63, 65
Petrarch 73, 75
Philip IV of France 70, *74*, 75
philosophy 145, 146
Pienza 118, *120*
pilgrimages 88
Pinturicchio *130–1*
Pius II, Pope 118, *119*, 127
Pius III, Pope 128, *130–1*
Pius IX, Pope *162*, *163*, *164–5*, 165–6
Pius XI, Pope 175, *176*, 179–80
Pius XII, Pope *180*, 181
Pizarro, Francisco *156–7*
plenary indulgences 85, 86, 88
Poland 181–4, *185*
Popiełuszko, Jerzy 182, 184, *185*
Portugal
    and the Inquisition 94, *108*, *109*
    and missionaries 153
    and the New World 109, 151, *152*
    and slavery 121, 123–4
Propaganda Due 192, 193
Protestantism 137–45, *141*, *142*
Prussian Crusade 55, 57
Pucci, Lorenzo 127–8
Pulitzer Prize 214
pure-bloodedness 105–6, *105*
Purgatory *82*, 85, 86–8

R
racial hygiene *105*, 105–6
rack 99
Raphael *24*, *116*, 132, *132*
Ratzinger, Joseph *see* Benedict XVI,
    Pope
Reformation
    in England 138–43
    in France 143
    in Germany 143–5
    in the Netherlands 143
relics 88–90, 137
Renaissance 112–33
Requirement, The 160, 162
Resurgence 165
resurrection *80*
Richard I, King of England 47, 49
Rimini, School of *8*
Roman Empire
    Christianity becomes official 25
    decline and fall 27–8, 31

early Christians 15–16, 19–23, 25
Edict Against the Christians 20
Edict of Toleration 25
invasions of 28
underground worship 21, 23
Roman Inquisition 109–11
Rome *10*
and the Borgias 121–9, *122*, *124–5*,
126, *128–9*
early Christians 15–16, 19–23, 25
East-West Schism 66, 68
Europa Multiclub 203
fire 16
and Innocent VIII, Pope 118, 120
invasions of 28, *35*
pilgrimages to 85
Popes and anti-Popes 65, 70, 75–6
Roman Empire 15–31
Sack of Rome 26, 133, *133*
underground worship 21, 23
Romero, Archbishop Oscar 187, *188–9*
Rosa, Enrico 181
Rousseau, Jean-Jacques 146
Rovere, Felice della 131, *132*
Rubens, Pieter Paul *17*
Russia 174–5, *175*

S

Sack of Rome *26*, 133, *133*
Saladin 47, 49, *49*
salvation *82*, 83–90
Saracens 37, 44, 49
Sassetti, Filippo 153
Saul 15–16
science 109–11, 145–6
Second Crusade 45, *46–7*
Second World War 181
Seljuk 41, *48*
Sepulveda, Juan Ginés de 161
sex
AIDS 206, *206*
birth control 205–6
celibacy 115, 118, 207–9
child abuse 210–17
early Christians 20–1
homosexuality 117, 203, 209
and Pius II, Pope 118
Siena cathedral *130–1*
Sigulda Castle *54*
simony 90, *91*
Sistine Chapel *136*
Sixtus IV, Pope *114*, 115, 117

slavery 121, 123–4
Smyth, Father Brendan *213*, 213–14
Society of Missionaries of Africa 168
South America *156–7*, 184, 186–7, *186*,
187, 207
Spain
al-Andalus 33, 103
Charles I of Spain 161, *161*
civil war 176, 179
Ferdinand and Isabella 102, *102*,
103, 105, 106
Franco, Francisco 176, *178*, 179
and the Inquisition 93–103, 105–9
and Jews 79, 105, 106, 109
Leyenda Negra 94, 97
and *Marranos* 109
martyrdom of objects 179
and Mexico 158–60
missionaries 155–6, 158–61
and the Moors 109
and Muslims 32, 33, 35, 49, 106,
108, 109
and the New World 108–9, 151, *152*,
155–61
and pure-bloodedness 105–6, *105*
and the Reformation 143
and slavery 123–4
Sprenger, Jakob 61
St Bartholomew's Day Massacre (1572)
144
St Patrick's College, Cavan 214
St Peter's basilica 135, 137
Stephen, Saint 15–16, *17*
Suetonius 16
Syllabus of Errors 165
Sylvester I, Pope *24*, 25
Syria 41, *42*, 43, 47, 49

T

Tacitus 16
Tariq ibn-Zayid *33*
Tedeschini, Federico *178*
Tenochtitlán 159, *159*, *160*
Teresa of Avila, Saint *104*
Teutonic Knights 55, *55*, 57
Theodosius I, Emperor 66, *67*
Theresa of Lisieux, Saint *9*
Third Crusade 47, 49
Thirty Years War 144
Tito, Marshal *170*, 171
Tordesillas, Treaty of 151, *152*
Torquemada, Tomás de 102, 106, *106*

torture, and the Inquisition 93–4, 97–9,
97, *98*, *99*, 106
Tours, Battle of (732) 32–3, *34*
Traditores 31
transubstantiation 57
Trujillo, Rafael 190
Turkey 38, 41, 66, 68–9, 195
Tyndale, William 137

U

Uganda 168, *169*
United States 190, 214, *215*, 216, *216*
Urban II, Pope *36*, 37–8, *39*
Urban VI, Pope 76, *76*

V

Valens, Emperor 28, *28*
Vatican *217*
and Pius IX, Pope 165
Secret Archives 13, *13*
and sovereign territory 25, 165, 175
Vatican Bank 188, 190–1
Vatican Council, First *164–5*, 165–6
Velázquez, Eugenio Lucas *107*
Veneto, Bartolomeo *126*
Victor Emmanuel, King of Italy *162*
Villa, Pancho 173
Virgin Mary, visions of 171, *172–3*, 173
Voltaire 146, *147*

W

Waldensians 57
Waldo, Peter 57, *57*
Watkins, Carl 88
Western Schism 76–9
Westminster Abbey 87–8
White Fathers 168
White Terror 176, 179
William of Norwich, Saint 53
Willshire, Vera 212–13
witchcraft 58, 61
Wojtyła, Karol *see* John Paul II, Pope
Wolsey, Thomas *139*, 140
Worms 41
Wycliffe, John 56, 57

Y

York, anti-Semitism 52
Yugoslavia *170*, 171, *172–3*

Z

Zapata, Emiliano 173, *174*

PICTURE CREDITS

AKG: 22

Alamy: 1 (Art Archive/Collection Dagli Orti), 2 (Art Archive/Gianni Dagli Orti), 7 (Art Archive/Gianni Dagli Orti), 9 (Photo 12), 14 (Interfoto), 17 (Art Gallery Collection), 18 (ASP Religion), 20 (Interfoto), 28 (Interfoto), 30 (Art Gallery Collection), 33 (Prisma Archivo), 45 (Art Gallery), 46 (Art Gallery), 48 (Stock Montage), 50 (TPM Photostock), 51 (Art Archive/Gianni Dagli Orti), 52 (Superstock), 55 (Interfoto), 57 (Interfoto), 60 (Robert Harding), 61 (Interfoto), 64 (Prisma Archivo), 65 (IAM), 68 (Glasshouse Images), 76 (Robert Harding), 78 (Interfoto), 80 (Art Gallery), 83 (Art Archive), 89 (North Wind), 91 (Timewatch), 92 (Art Archive/ Gianni Dagli Orti), 96 (Prisma Archivo), 100 (Prisma Archivo), 102 (Everett Collection), 103 (IAM), 106 (IAM), 108 (Print Collector), 120 (Universal Images Group), 123 (Everett Collection), 126 (GL Archive), 132 (SuperStock), 133 (Emilio Ereza), 139 (HIP), 144 (Art Archive/Gianni Dagli Orti), 147 (Nick Fielding), 148 (Classic Image), 150 (Nikreates), 152 (Art Archive/Gianni Dagli Orti), 201 (FMD), 204 (Friedrich Stark), 210 (Bettina Strenske)

Corbis: 6 (Reuters/Parth Sanyal), 8 (Arte & Immagini), 10 (Gianni Dagli Orti), 11 (Tim Graham), 12 (Reuters/ Nir Elias), 13 (Ted Spigel), 15 (Print Collector), 23 (Robert Harding), 24 (Burstein Collection), 27 (Alinari Archives), 29 (Francis G. Mayer), 35 (Fine Art), 40 (Stefano Bianchetti), 41 (Christel Gerstenberg), 42 (Leonard de Selva), 44 (Chris Hellier), 49 (Leonard de Selva), 56 (Lebrecht), 62 (Art Archive/Gianni Dagli Orti), 74 (Stapleton Collection), 77 (Tarker), 79 (Stefano Bianchetti), 81 (Araldo de Luca), 82 (Alinari), 86 (Gallery Collection), 99 (Ali Meyer), 104 (Heritage Images), 105 (Brooklyn Museum), 116 (National Gallery), 134 (Tarker), 135 (Fine Art), 136 (Stefano Bianchetti), 140 (HIP), 145 (Art Archive/Dagli Orti), 146 (PoodlesRock), 149 (Art Archive/Alfredo Dagli Orti), 153 (Reuters/Arko Datta), 156 (Fine Art), 158 (J.L. Kraemer), 159 (Gallery Collection), 162, 172 (Reuters), 175 (National Geographic Society), 180 (Hulton), 184 (Sygma/Gianni Giansanti), 185 (Reuters/Wojciech Olkusnik), 186 (Horacio Villalobos), 187 (Horacio Villalobos), 191 (Hulton), 193 (ANSA), 198 (Demotix/Adele King), 199 (Splash News), 200 (Demotix/Art Widak), 202 (EPA/STF), 206 (EPA/Nic Bothma), 207 (Sygma/Rick Maiman), 208 (Reuters/ Max Rossi), 209 (EPA/Guido Montani), 211 (Reuters), 215 (Reuters/David McNew), 216 (Reuters/Jonathan Ernst), 217 (Reuters/Observatore Romano)

Corbis/Bettmann: 19, 21, 26, 59, 67, 88, 121, 142, 160, 170, 171, 182, 188, 189, 194, 195

Dreamstime: 72 (Gunold Brumbauer)

Getty: 54 (Universal Images Group), 70 (De Agostini), 71 (Hulton), 84 (Roger-Viollet), 87 (National Geographic), 98 (De Agostini), 107 (Bridgeman), 122 (Universal Images Group), 128 (DEA/Bardazzi), 130 (Lonely Planet Images/ Roberto Gerometta), 138 (British Library), 168 (Bridgeman), 169 (Time & Life/ David Lees), 177 (Hulton), 178 (Time & Life/Dmitir Kessel), 190 (AFP), 192 (AFP), 196 (AFP/Andreas Solaro), 197 (AFP/Vincenzo Pinto), 212 (Joe Dunne)

Library of Congress: 5, 37, 63, 109, 163, 164, 174

Mary Evans Picture Library: 53, 66, 95, 97, 110, 112, 114, 117, 119, 124, 125, 141, 154, 155, 161, 167, 176

Newscom: 36 (AKG)

Photos.com: 34, 39, 93, 113

Press Association: 213 (Brian Little)